CW01337983

Spitfires Reborn

SPITFIRES REBORN

By
David Green

Brooks Books
England

Copyright ©David Green & Brooks Books 1991

Published in Great Britain by Brooks Books, 23 Sylvan Avenue, Bitterne, Southampton, Hampshire, SO2 5JW, England.

British Library Cataloguing in Publication Data

Available from the British Library on request.

ISBN 1 872706 12 6

All rights reserved. No part of this publication may be reproduced, stored in a retrieval system or transmitted in any form or by any means, electronic, mechanical, photocopying, recording or otherwise, without the prior written permission of the copyright owner.

Printed in the Channel Islands by the Guernsey Press.

CONTENTS

Prologue (9)
1. The Battle of Britain Memorial Flight (13)
2. A Bonny, Wee Scot (43)
3. Spitfires Down Under (53)
4. The Two Graces (63)
5. The Micheldever Story (81)
6. Spitfires and Saviours (97)
This is Not the End (127)

Acknowledgements

The author wishes to acknowledge with thanks, the help and support given him by the following:

Air Vice Marshal J. E. ('Johnnie') Johnson CB CBE DSO DFC DL for his kindness in interrupting a busy life to contribute the foreword.

Sqn. Ldr. Colin Paterson, the officer commanding the Battle of Britain Memorial Flight, Sqn. Ldr. Paul Day AFC, the Senior and Junior NCOs and Airmen of the Flight.

Gp. Capt. Hamish Mahaddie DSO DFC AFC CZMC C Eng FRAeS for his friendship and a dram.

Mrs Carolyn Grace, for allowing me to tell the story of 'The Two Graces'.

Mrs S. Church, who permitted me to tell 'The Micheldever Story'.

Dick and Carol Melton for their good-humoured co-operation.

All at Aerofab for their help and advice now and in times past.

Flt. Lt. Don Healey for his unfailing support.

Peter Arnold, historian, photographer, engineer and sleuth, for the friendly support he has always given to the author and the Spitfire Society.

Particular thanks are owed to my long-suffering companions who are officers of the Executive Committee of the Spitfire Society – Gurney Smeed, Peter Clarke, Reg Saffin, Bill Williams, (who supplied the cover photo) Tony Howard, Dennis Williams, George Bromley, Peter and Peggy Allen, Tony White, and to Bert Chivers. Finally, a million thanks to their even longer-suffering wives and families.

To my own wife, Diana, who has put up with my obsession concerning flying – machines and people – for the last forty-one years – what can I say? Just 'Thank you' I suppose – and 'I won't do it again.' (but I will).

Bibiliography

Flypast and Aeroplane Monthly over the years

MT719 – A Spitfire MkVIII – Keith Hiscock

Strive to Excel – Keith Hiscock

Squadron Codes – Bowyer and Rawlings

Battle of Britain – Leonard Moseley

Hamish – The Story of a Pathfinder – Mahaddie

Spitfire – The Story of a Famous Fighter – Bruce Robertson

Pilot's Notes for Spitfire – A. P. 1565

Foreword

Men came from every corner of the world to fly and fight in Spitfires, and on the morning of 15th September 1940, when the Battle of Britain was reaching its climax, the invaders were met, fought and harried by an outstanding and diverse gathering of fighting men—perhaps the most outstanding ever to defend our shores. They were led into the hostile regions by squadron, flight and section leaders, many of whom, for the past few months, had fought continuously over France, Dunkirk, the Channel and Southern England. Now they were seasoned air fighters who had the advantage of flying over their own country and defending their homeland. Skilled air fighters from the Empire — South Africa, Rhodesia, Canada, Australia and New Zealand — defending the 'Old Country' which still had a very real meaning and significance for them. Veteran air fighters, not of their own kith and kin, but from Poland, Czechoslovakia, Norway, France, Holland and Belgium, some of whom had fought, since the autumn of 1939, in three Air Forces and had old and bitter scores to settle — and little to lose.

The Battle of Britain was won because we had good aeroplanes and good leaders. There were more Hurricane than Spitfire squadrons, but the latter was the only Allied fighter to remain in production throughout the war; no less than 22,759 Spitfires and seafires were built in some 52 operational variants.

Today, there are but a handful left, and in his splendid book, the founder of our Spitfire Society tells you where you may see Mitchell's elegant fighter and hear again her Merlin's song of freedom.

Air Vice-Marshal 'Johnnie' Johnson.
CB CBE DSO DFC DL

PROLOGUE

22nd January, 1951.

The orange orb of the sinking sun rested temporarily on the purple-grey ridges of the hills along the western shores of Port Shelter, one of the many inlets probing northwards into the New Territories of Hong Kong. The rocket and air-to-ground gunnery targets, sited on a thin spit of sand and rock, were already enveloped in the shadows of the evening. The sampans, with their ragged crews of boat people which had, as usual, been standing by all day close — much too close — to the targets to salvage the expended shell-cases ejected from the aircraft, hoisted their tattered sails of canvas and bamboo and drifted slowly away towards the Kowloon typhoon shelters.

Climbing away from the targets I cleaned up the cockpit; gyro gunsight off, gun button to safe, all other armament switches off. Revelling in the cool, calm evening air I made one more low, fast run past the Range Safety Officer's quadrant to waggle a 'goodnight and thanks' before returning to our airstrip at Sek Kong. I was already too late. Guy Mott, our affable Canadian Wing Weapons Officer, had locked up and left, en route for his first comforting libation of the evening on the balcony of the gracious Officers' Mess at Kai Tak, overlooking the airfield and harbour.

I turned northwards towards our airstrip, out in the sticks, a couple of miles south of the Communist Chinese border — the Bamboo Curtain as it had been dubbed. It consisted of PSP (Pierced steel Planking), linked metal strips laid over drained and graded one-time paddy fields. Sek Kong sheltered in the immediate lee of the great

Spitfires Reborn

bulk of Tai Mo Shan, the highest peak in the Territories at some 3,000 feet. It completely dominated the airstrip, shortly to be closed in order to lay a more permanent runway and parking apron in readiness to receive our brand-new *de Havilland Vampire* single-seater jet fighters.

I viewed the forthcoming change with mixed feelings. Almost exactly ten years previously, on 23rd January 1941, I had made my first acquaintance with the *Supermarine Spitfire*. My lord and mentor sent me off on that dank morning in a battered *Mark 1* to 'find out all about it — and don't bloody well bend it!'. Well, I didn't, and in the intervening years I had spent a great amount of time with the *Spitfire* as my sole companion. I now found it difficult to imagine a world without it.

Ah, well, if change was inevitable, no doubt I would be able to relax and enjoy it. I throttled back, and the mighty Rolls Royce *Griffon's* tone reduced from its steady bellow to a complaining, low-pitched throaty grumble. With the canopy winched fully open, the wheels thumped down and the all-or-nothing ninety degrees of flap rapidly slowed our combined weight of nearly five tons to the initial approach speed of 140 knots. I brought my aircraft 'Echo' round the tightish turn necessitated by the surrounding hills to curve on to the final approach towards the mountain.

The last moments of 'holding off' came as the long, sleek nose came up and up, obscuring all forward vision. The aircraft sank to the ground, and the metallic protests of the runway sharply reminded one that the flight would only be over once the engine had been stopped in dispersal. With an intermittent hissing of the pneumatic braking system the Echo slowed, and the cacophony of the metal strips died away to a staccato murmur.

Flaps up and access door open for improved forward vision, we headed for the marshaller. I was the last to return, and he would be impatient to get off for his tea in the Airmens' Mess. In answer to his signals I turned Echo into position and, with a final look around, pulled back the fuel cut-off lever. Almost immediately the engine faded into silence, and the five awesome blades of the propeller whirred to a stop.

As the marshaller dragged the wooden chocks into position beneath the wheels I unstrapped and jumped to the ground. Divesting

Prologue

myself of the cumbersome parachute and dinghy I reflected that, probably for the last time, I was about to walk away from my beloved *Spitfire*, that forgiving friend with which I had shared so many adventures for almost a decade.

I found the thought distasteful, and I was unwilling to accept the reality. But, deep down, I knew it was the parting of the ways. Some of our aircraft had already gone to Kai Tak to await their fate, and I knew that the Chinese scrap metal merchants were even now enjoying their haggling over the few remaining *Spitfire Mk XVIIIs* — including Echo. Meanwhile, down south in Singapore, our shiny new *Vampires* awaited our collection.

The sun had now sunk below the horizon and the valley was filled with the purple shadows of evening. Here and there pinpricks of flame and smudges of wood smoke on the hillsides forecast that the evening chow was on its way. The last, familiar smells and tickings of a cooling engine wafted away on the light evening breeze.

I walked away from Echo towards the crew-room and the *Austin* 2-tonner which would return me to my home in Kowloon. I passed beneath the aircraft's nose, thinking that somehow, our farewell was all too casual — that I was being cavalier and uncaring.

Then — the author as 'A' Flight Commander, Green 73 Squadron, Malta, 1945 (Green)

Sentimental nonsense, of course. Aircraft are aircraft, metal fashioned by man for specific purposes. But I remember thinking that

Spitfires Reborn

this was, in fact, a very real watershed. That *Spitfires,* the fighter bastions of every theatre of World War 2, long gone from the home-based RAF, were about to depart the flying scene for ever.

As we shall see, I was wrong. Much later, another generation of enthusiasts with a strong sense of heritage would recognise the beauty and value of those machines. With determination and painstaking work they would ensure that the British public, and the world at large, would not be allowed to forget this great fighter aircraft which did everything it had to do when it was most needed.

This book is about today's *Spitfire* people, and some of the aircraft which have been rescued from oblivion.

Now — DJG with the Shuttleworth Collection Spitfire Mk V. BL628, 1988.

CHAPTER ONE

The Battle of Britain Memorial Flight

The History.

Some six years after I walked away from *Echo* at far-off Sek Kong I found myself, as they say, 'flying a desk'. Having moved into the world of jets (pretty tame stuff, I thought, after the big pistons) I had made the long voyage back to the UK with Diana and our one-year-old Julia, in the redoubtable *Empire Windrush* — a vessel with a very chequered history.

A one-time Nazi 'strength-through-joy' ship she had, it was said, twice been dispatched to the bottom of the sea by RAF bombs. It was in that condition that she was finally discovered by the British occupying forces. They raised her for the second time, cleared her of barnacles and seaweed, and declared her fit to become a troopship on the Far East run. Captain Wilson, her Master, was a gentleman of character who had made his own assessment of the reliability of his vessel, ran things with a single-minded observance of discipline. He had himself been the victim of two torpedo attacks and he was fairly certain that the *Empire Windrush* (or *Imperial Fart* as she was irreverently known by the troops), would, if allowed, put the final nail in his coffin. He was not far wrong, for a couple of trips later her engine-room blew up and the ship went to the bottom for the third and last time—fortunately with the loss of only four lives. Captain Wilson survived to hang up his sea-boots in peaceful retirement.

A contented three years as a flying instructor with Oxford University Air Squadron followed our return to the homeland. Then, unexpectedly as far as I was concerned, I was kicked upstairs to Squadron Leader—and straight out of the cockpit to become chairborne behind a desk.

The only discernable compensations for that turn of fate were that I had an increase in salary (to around seventy-five pounds per month), the task was interesting, and I was at the hub of the fighter world as I had been appointed Command Flight Safety Officer at Fighter Command Headquarters, RAF Bentley Priory. It is not part of this narrative to describe the various vicissitudes which accompanied such a job beyond saying that, in 1956, after a decade or so of jet experience the RAF's move into the second generation of front-line fighters *(Hunters* and *Javelins)* was not proceeding entirely without incident. In short, as the Command's chief investigator of things that went bump in the night—and day—I was being kept fully occupied.

In such a demanding role it is easy, by the very nature of one's daily round, to develop an aura of gloom. It is in no-one's interests to allow that to occur. Consequently I, and my principal assistant and old friend from Hong Kong days, Cedric Simons, waged a constant and determined battle to rise above the steady tide of bad news.

One bright summer day in July, 1957, in our dingy office, where the brightest of the sun's rays never penetrated, I threw my over-used ball-point into the general clutter of the desk. For more than a year I had waded my way through every last detail of Boards of Inquiry into dozens of aircraft accidents, and written tens of thousands of words about them. Some light relief was called for.

My eyes had just rested momentarily on the front page of that excellent journal, the Royal Air Force News. The front page headline read:'Battle of Britain Flight Formed'. The story reported the arrival at RAF Biggin Hill (an historic Fighter Command base) of three *Spitfire Mk XIX* aircraft to join what had been known until then as the Air Historic Flight.

The origins of that diminutive unit went back to 15th September 1945 — later to become known as Battle of Britain Day. Then, the end of the war was marked by a great fly-past over London which included hundreds of fighters of the RAF and Allied air forces. In subsequent years it was considered fitting to repeat the commemoration, although on a decreased scale. Naturally, it was appropriate that on each occasion the event should be led by the two main RAF protagonists of the Battle of Britain, the *Hurricane* and the *Spitfire*.

From 1945 onwards the great days of the *Hurricane* were over, although a number of *Spitfires* remained on the scene for a few further years. This, clearly, created a problem where the fly-past was concerned, and posed more trouble in future years where *Spitfires* were concerned. With a commendable, and somewhat rare sense of history, a single *Hurricane* was retained in service. The old warrior had somehow been preserved in a flyable condition despite, one imagines, the disapproval of the financiers to whom subjective arguments were anathema no matter how small the sum of money involved. In their view, anything that had no positive value in the front line or as a training vehicle was fit only for the knacker's yard.

Nevertheless, every year from 1945 onwards the fly-past over the nation's capital had been led by the venerable *Hurricane*, properly partnered whenever possible by its one-time comrade in battle, a *Spitfire*. The Battle of Britain Commemorative Fly-past, as it had come to be known, evoked sighs of thanks and nostalgia as the citizens of London, many of whom had experienced the ravages of war all too closely, turned their eyes skywards and remembered.

As had been foreseen by some, that annual achievement became ever more difficult to accomplish. With no establishment of manpower or logistics the precious *Hurricane* presented an increasing burden as the years ticked by. Furthermore, as Fighter Command's Order of Battle became ever more jet-powered, *Spitfires* became, firstly, an endangered species, and then, by the mid-50s, virtually extinct. The last source, the Army co-operation squadrons, either re-equipped or were disbanded in the early '50s, when their duties were handed over to civilian contractors. Some remaining *Spitfires* were stored, often in the open with little or no protection. Others were allocated to various bases to act as 'gate guardians'. Some were sold at knock-down prices to foreign air forces, some regaining their independence after enemy occupation, others emerging as a result of the dismemberment of empires, including the British. Untold numbers were sold to the army of scrap dealers abounding at that time.

With a lone *Hurricane* surviving to equip the Air Historic Flight its future, by 1956, must have seemed to be bleak indeed. Ten years after the war's end, with the nation struggling to keep its head above the flood of threatening political, industrial and commercial issues, when it would have been so easy to allow the concept to simply fade away.

Fortunately, there were many wartime aircrew still serving in the RAF who were disinclined to allow such a thing to occur. In particular, there were a number of veterans of the Battle of Britain and many other ensuing air actions who had, over the years, attained senior rank in positions of influence within the Air Ministry and Fighter Command. Such people were sufficiently far-sighted to recognise the importance of safeguarding 'living' examples of the nation's military heritage. They were also unlikely to be daunted by unimaginative arguments concerned with gleaning a pieces of silver in exchange for real history.

Already the destruction of the RAF's now functionally outdated equipment was well advanced. By 1953, not a single *Short Stirling* existed; a handful of *Handley-Page Halifax* bombers had either been 'civilianised' or passed into foreign hands; Hundreds of *Lancasters* were lined up in the exposed fields of Wiltshire and East Anglia awaiting their turn to be put down.

Things came to a head when the last coherent body to operate *Spitfires* came under the scrutiny of the financiers. This was the unique, so-called THUM Flight (the acronym was derived from the words temperature and humidity), a civilian-operated unit based at Woodvale, Lancashire. Its task had been to make daily observation flights in *Spitfire PR Mk XIXs* to provide data for the Meteorological Office. The need for such a specialised body had declined by the mid-50s in the light of advancing technologies. The inevitable decision was taken to disband its activities in 1957, thus bringing to an end the last operational function of RAF Spitfires anywhere in the world. It was twenty years, including a world war, since 19 Squadron had received its first *Spitfire Mk Is*.

The Battle of Britain Memorial Flight

Fortunately, good sense prevailed. In early June, 1957, the last meteorological readings were taken, and the three pale blue *Spitfires* were prepared for their short flight in the hands of their civilian pilots to RAF Duxford, where they were to be handed back to their parent Service. Two arrived there on 14th June. The third *(PS853)* was a reluctant starter when it ran out of runway and ended up on its nose. (One wonders if the old *Spitfire* cry of: 'There 'e goes, on 'is nose, got 'is brakes on, I suppose' was heard again for the last time). No serious damage had been done, and *PS853* rejoined her companions at Duxford on 26th June, 1957.

By 11th July all was ready for what had now become something of a 'welcome home' flight, to join the lone *Hurricane* of the Historic Aircraft Flight at Biggin Hill. Fittingly, the *Spitfires* were flown on that memorable occasion by Group Captain (later Air Vice-Marshal) 'Johnnie' Johnson, Group Captain 'Jamie' Rankin, and Wing Commander Peter Thompson.

It was entirely appropriate that the three veteran aircraft, after six years in civilian hands, should have been properly greeted by the RAF. An escort was provided by three *Hawker Hunters* and three *Gloster Javelins* representing the front line squadrons of Fighter Command.

So it was that, within days of the formation of what had now become officially known as the Battle of Britain Flight (and the Command having had a run of several accident-free days), I said to Cedric, "Let us arise and go now. For once again there are *Spitfires* to be seen within Fighter Command. It behoves us, as diligent staff officers, to remove ourselves to Biggin Hill where we shall study all relevant flight safety aspects." And, I could have added, remake our acquaintance with the classic shape, sound and smell of what I still regarded as a 'real' aeroplane.

As we stood outside a lonely hangar on the far side of that airfield—itself a hallowed survivor of the Battle of Britain—*Hawker Hunters* thundered down the runway and out over the valley, or whistled sleekly around the circuit. I gazed at the newly arrived *Spitfire XIXs* and thought: Thank Heavens for the foresight which saved these beauties from the torch.

But it had been a close-run thing. Who could have known what future cases would need to be fought to preserve those ageing aircraft, and the newly-formed Battle of Britain Flight itself? For their presence had depended, in the end, on an inarticulate, undefinable groundswell of feeling within the RAF. It had arisen from the awful impropriety, the unseemliness, of the thoughtless destruction of machines which, a few years before, had born our young aircrews into battle and won the day.

The survival of these aircraft, I reflected, had not been a matter of rescuing rusting hulks from disintegration. They were here because someone, somewhere, (doubtless a much maligned staff officer) had the foresight and imagination to keep them alive. Whoever he was, he had, in fact, been the founder of probably the first example of what today's jargon would label a 'theme exhibition'.

That is why the Battle of Britain Memorial Flight deserves the place of honour in this fascinating story of surviving *Spitfires*. Ever since that September day in 1945, when the first-ever thanksgiving fly-past made its way over Tower Bridge, Westminster and along the Mall to Buckingham Palace, the RAF has been proud to carry out its mission to preserve and protect our aviation heritage. For thirty-four years the Flight has carried out its task—often threatened by political or financial circumstances—but because of its dedication and good husbandry it is with us yet.

Supported now by a multitude of today's enthusiasts, mostly unborn when the aircraft first rolled out into the light of a wartime day, and by a more enlightened attitude on the part of officialdom, it is to be hoped that the BBMF (as it is now widely known) faces a secure future.

The Battle of Britain Memorial Flight—The Aircraft.

The Battle of Britain Memorial Flight is an established unit of the Royal Air Force. Its home base is at RAF Coningsby, Lincolnshire. There, close to the northern boundary of the airfield, the great, brick-built Keep of what had once been Tattershall Castle, a survivor of 550 years, stands four-square against the thunder of the *Tornadoes* which also occupy the base.

The Battle of Britain Memorial Flight

Since those early days at Biggin Hill, when its Spitfires had first touched down after their flight from Duxford in 1957, much has been added to the continuing story of the BBMF.

No sooner had the Flight become established itself at Biggin Hill than it became the subjected to almost constant change. It was not alone. Throughout the decade of the '50s, the RAF as a whole was re-designing itself to meet its new Cold War responsibilities. It was introducing new operational concepts and equipment, learning to live within NATO, and, yet, trimming itself to enable its tightly monitored sources to stretch a long way. It was, indeed, an era of change for a defence force which still retained global commitments, particularly in the Far East, the Gulf and the Mediterranean. Simultaneously, costs escalated, and the severely limited funds shared by the three Services, each one convinced that its role in the air, on land or on sea, qualified it for the lion's share.

Against such a background the BBMF's very existence was indeed precarious. It kept a low profile, demanding nothing, improvising where necessary, and nurturing the benevolent encouragement of people in high places.

Within a few weeks one of the ex-Woodvale trio, *PS915*, had shown herself (*Spitfires* are always feminine) to be such an unpredictable performer that she was given up for lost where flying was concerned. She was 'struck off' the Flight's strength and dispatched to RAF West Malling, near Maidstone, Kent, to stand silent guard at the main gate. Her flying days were over — or were they?

The Flight had to make do with two *Spitfires* for a only a brief period. Later in 1957 a brace of *Spitfire Mk XVIs* turned up in London to add a little style to the Royal Tournament. When the final curtain fell on that year's exhibition of military histrionics the two aircraft materialised at Biggin Hill. The manner of their movement is lost in the mists of time — but there they were, and possession is nine-tenths of the law. The Station Commander, Squadron Leader R S Salmon, was presiding over Biggin Hill's last twelve months as a fighter station. A busy man, no doubt, who was only at the threshold of senior rank, he nevertheless distinguished himself by decreeing that the two *Mk XVIs* should be made fit to fly.

There was just enough time left to accomplish that task before the Air Ministry ordered the closure of the airfield. Consequently,

Spitfires Reborn

the Flight packed up and moved to RAF North Weald – another fighter station to the north of London which had once been heavily engaged in the air defence of the capital. At that time the BBMF was equipped with the lone *Hurricane*, the two *Spitfire Mk XIXs*, and the newly acquired *Spitfire Mk XVIs*.

There was to be no peace. The year 1958 will always be remembered by servicemen as a time of great turbulence. Just one year previously, on 4th April 1957, a Defence White Paper had appeared over the signature of Duncan Sandys which had been so sweeping that the RAF, in particular, was to be fundamentally affected for a long time to come. Baldly and briefly, the document set out to change totally the existing air defence system of Great Britain. Unmanned guided weapons, said Sandys, would take over the country's aerial defence. The prime responsibility of Fighter Command – indeed, virtually its sole remaining task – would be the protection of the nation's nuclear deterrent in the shape of Bomber Command's V-Force – the *Valiants, Victors* and *Vulcans*.

Just one effect of that policy was the almost 100% redeployment or disbanding of existing home defence forces. The Battle of Britain Flight, suspended by a thread for its very existence, was probably the last consideration to occupy the thoughts of Fighter Command's Commander-in-Chief, Air Chief Marshal Sir Thomas Pike.

Hardly had the Flight had time to unpack its tool-kits when the news came through that North Weald, too, was to close. But not before the Flight had suffered a further loss of a second *Spitfire XIX*, when the extraordinary decision had been taken to allocate that serviceable aircraft to RAF West Raynham – as a gate guardian! That is an apt illustration of the wavering of purpose which the Sandys White Paper had engendered throughout the RAF. The gesture was singularly inappropriate, in any case. At that time West Raynham was home to the Central Fighter Establishment, a centre of tactical research and post-graduate training – and here was some faceless staff officer or civil servant presenting it with a photographic reconnaissance aircraft. Lovely though it may have been, the *Spitfire Mk XIX* had never been armed with anything more lethal than a battery of cameras! Fortunately, there was someone at West Raynham who had sufficient regard for the aircraft to see that it was, in fact, kept in flying condition – a circumstance for which the Battle of Britain

Memorial Flight would be most grateful some years later. In the meantime, the aircraft was flown from time to time by the staff pilots of Central Flying Establishment.

Once again, the little unit philosophically packed its bags and moved itself off—this time to RAF Martlesham Heath, Suffolk. On 20th September 1959 the *Hurricane* and one of the *Spitfire Mk XVIs* set off to lead the annual fly-past. The *Spitfire* was being flown by a very senior officer who, nineteen years previously, had fought in those same late summer skies over south-east England.

Alas, misfortune in the flying game recognises no dignity of rank. The pleasure of that flight of nostalgia was suddenly rudely shattered when the *Packard Merlin* of the *Mk XVI* shuddered into silence. As ceremonial fly-pasts were usually flown at no more than fifteen hundred feet above ground level there was very little time for the pilot to assess the situation in order to achieve a fairly dignified arrival back to Mother Earth. A further complication arose because his stricken *Spitfire*, being rapidly overtaken by a large number of jet fighters, was suspended momentarily and motorless, over the southern suburbs of London on a busy Saturday afternoon.

Having done all he could in the cockpit to prepare his aircraft for the inevitable crash (because of the vast urban spread beneath there was no question of taking to his parachute) the pilot selected his only option for a forced landing. It was the Oxo Co's cricket ground at Bromley, Kent.

One can imagine the startled countenances of all present—particularly the umpires, whose duty it is to adjudicate on such matters—when a *Spitfire* arrived on the scene at 100 plus miles per hour over the sidescreen. Happily, cricketers in the field are quick off the mark, and our gallant and experienced pilot did all that was required of him. The aircraft settled gently on the greensward amidst a splintering of airscrew blades and flying turf, and slid to a standstill. The pilot climbed out none the worse for his adventure. The cricket match was declared a draw ("Plane stopped play"), and all repaired to the pavilion bar.

As bad luck would have it, the second *Spitfire Mk XVI* had suffered a landing accident some days previously. The easy decision was quickly made. Neither aircraft ever flew again.

Spitfires Reborn

The Flight settled in at Martlesham Heath leading a fairly hand-to-mouth existence with its miraculously surviving *Hurricane* and the remaining *Spitfire Mk XIX*. Its future under almost constant review, the little unit struggled on. Since the write-offs of the two *Mk XVIs* the Flight was no longer able to quote the annual fly-past as a reason for its continuance. After the accident at Bromley the two venerable aircraft had been banned from the skies over London in the interests of safety.

Occasionally, one or other of the old fighters would appear fleetingly at some function or another, and a few hearts would beat a little faster, but these were doldrum days, and the very few officers in Fighter Command Headquarters (of whom the author was one) would not have been prepared to bet too much on the Flight's long-term future.

The late '50s were years of economic stringency. They were also years of revolutionary and expensive developments within the RAF. The very raison d'etre of the Service had changed drastically with its guardianship of the national nuclear deterrent — that responsibility bringing with it the V-bomber fleets, modernised high security bases, and an enormous range of tailor-made infrastructure. From the focal centre of the V-force the waves spread outwards. Squadrons of *Thor* intercontinental ballistic missiles were created. The air defence of the strike bases entered the world of push-button technology when *Bloodhound* guided weapons were deployed to join the existing squadrons of manned fighters. Sophisticated Sector Operations Centres were constructed deep underground.

The training of aircrews and groundcrews to match the new equipment with its extended capabilities needed to be entirely revamped and accelerated. But the years had passed quickly. Despite all those bewildering developments in the world of defence, it was only a matter of just over ten years since the Second World War had come to an end, and just six or seven since the last *Spitfires* had been phased out of the front line of the RAF. The gradual transfer of interest from the contemporary to the historic was still incomplete. Neither aviators nor the interested public had as yet firmly placed the last of the piston-engined fighters firmly into the past.

For the same reason, there was little appreciation shown by non-military aviation buffs that, very soon, the discarded weaponry of a world war would become valuable trophies and show-pieces. It was still so much scrap, flotsam available for the making of a fast buck through its destruction. Today's all-embracing air pageants, with their set-piece displays of vintage aircraft as performers in their own right, were virtually unknown in the '50s, and such as there were, had certainly not attracted the dozens of entrepreneurs now involved in bringing the aviation past back to life.

Against all that background of rapid development and activity, and the lack of realisation that the aviation world would inevitably evolve its own branch of military history, it is hardly surprising that there was virtually no time, money or effort to spare within the RAF to do more than keep the Battle of Britain Flight in existence, almost in name only, with the willing assistance of a few volunteers. Beyond that, the Service was only able to commemorate its recent past victories by standing the more presentable examples of its erstwhile fighting aircraft at the main gates of its bases, in the grounds of its various headquarters, and in a few ad hoc museums around the country. No establishment of maintenance personnel, or any extra funding, was made for the upkeep of these survivors. It is only recently that, after years of weathering in the unkind climate of this country, that a sense of pride (or, perhaps, shame) has taken advantage of the technique of glass reinforced plastic to replace the weathered relics by convincing full-scale facsimiles. Examples may be seen at the RAF Museum, Hendon, and Biggin Hill, to name but two.

Let us return to our main theme. After almost four lean years at Martlesham Heath, what was left of the Flight was once again moved on. This time its new home was to be Horsham St. Faith (now Norwich Airport). The move coincided with the slightest upturn in the unit's fortunes, with rather more interest being evident here that there might be jam tomorrow if not today. It is true that no more aircraft joined the representative pair, but during the eighteen months sojourn at Horsham St. Faith a growing recognition of the Battle of Britain Flight's rightful place in the order of things began to emerge. Perhaps this was because the RAF itself had celebrated its first forty years of independence in 1969, and was at last gaining confidence in its own traditions and heritage. Perhaps with the tu-

Spitfires Reborn

multuous and morale-sapping years of the '50s thankfully slipping into memory, together with the political disbandment of overseas Commands, there was a little more time and effort to devote to a re-appraisal of priorities. Perhaps, indeed, there was someone, or group, of influential people at Horsham St.Faith prepared to take a greater interest in the affairs of the little unit putting up such a gallant struggle to remain in being.

Whatever the reasons, the Flight survived the closure of Horsham St. Faith and, on 1st April, 1963, (the forty-fourth birthday of the RAF) the *Hurricane* and *Spitfire* flew into their new home at RAF Coltishall, also near Norwich.

The long and the short of it! Two Spitfires of the BBMF with Concorde, Biggin Hill 1989. (Green)

What must have seemed a body-blow to the Flight some five years previously at North Weald, when *Spitfire Mk XIX PS583* had been transferred to West Raynham, was, after all to be revenged. As we have seen, she had mercifully never really become a static gate guardian. By hook or by crook the admittedly powerful authorities at the Central Fighter Establishment, with their direct links to Fighter Command Headquarters itself, had contrived to keep the aircraft in flying condition.

The Battle of Britain Memorial Flight

At last, good sense prevailed. The valuable survivor returned to the fold in April, 1964, there to form a much more respectable threesome. During the remainder of that year, the aircraft of the Battle of Britain Flight were seen at no less than fifty air and other displays across the country. Things were looking up.

There was, outside the RAF, one other evader of the scrapheap. *Spitfire MkVB AB910* – apart from one bizarre flight – had a wartime history which was more or less typical of the other 499 ordered from the giant 'shadow' factory at Castle Bromwich, Birmingham, on 22nd June 1940. The contract, in fact, had been for 500 *Mk Is,* but production coincided with the availability of the more powerful Rolls Royce *Merlin 45* engine (1,470 hp) with the consequence that the complete batch emerged as *Mk Vs.*

AB910 experienced a fairly normal wartime career, with much shuffling between front line squadrons and maintenance units. She served with the British, (Nos 222, 130 and 242 Sqns.), the Americans, (No 133 (Eagle) Sqn.), and the Canadians (Nos 416 and 402 Sqns.). During her time with the Eagle Sqn. *AB910* was involved in combat over Dieppe, her guns destroying a *Dornier 217*, and a part share in the destruction of a *FW 190*.

The aircraft also did a stint at No 53 Operational Training Unit, RAF Hibaldstow, near Brigg, Yorkshire. Aircraft on the strength of those units really earned their keep without any of the glamour. There were, and still are, some who are too ready to cast doubts on the ruggedness of the *Spitfire*. The relatively safe operation of those aircraft allocated to operational training, at a high utilisation rate, in the hands of young, inexperienced pilots, usually flying off poorly drained grass surfaces, should disabuse the doubters.

But they did have their moments. *AB910* was put to the test on one occasion when an incident occurred which is now part of RAF folklore. When running-up an engine, or taxying through soft ground, it was necessary to weight the tail to prevent it from rising under increased power with the aircraft in a braked condition. Such an occurrence, of course, would have a literally shattering effect on the propeller. The extra weight was provided by whatever luckless airmen or airwomen who happened to be available at the time. Their task was to lay themselves across the spine of the fuselage adjacent to the vertical fin thus providing a maximum anchoring effect.

On one occasion at Hibaldstow, Flt Lt Neil Cox was detailed to fly *AB910* on a local training flight. Immediately prior to take-off from that grass field he called for assistance in the manner described. one of the 'volunteers' stepped forward in the shape of Leading Aircraftswoman Margaret Horton, who obligingly spreadeagled her overalled body across the rear fuselage. The pilot successfully completed whatever operation he had been conducting and, without more ado, turned the aircraft into wind, opened up to full power, and took off.

During the process, he thought that the acceleration was not quite as lively as it should have been, and the attitude seemed rather tail-down. However, the aircraft left the ground safely enough, and Cox carried out his after take-off checks as normal. What was not normal was the fore-and-aft trim of *AB910*. To err on the safe side, the pilot decided to take the aircraft back for checking. He completed a circuit of the airfield at the circuit height of 1,000 feet, carried out the regulation *Spitfire* curved approach, followed by a pleasingly smooth landing.

Finally, as the aircraft drifted to a halt, Margaret Holton slid to the ground (for she had accompanied the aircraft throughout its flight, hanging on like grim death), and approached the cockpit. The pilot (so the story goes) turned to her quite calmly to say that he was about to put the aircraft unserviceable due to its tail-heaviness. Margaret's reply was not recorded, but she lived to recount that story on many an occasion in years to come.

AB910's stay at 57 OTU came to an end on 17th May, 1945, when she was re-allocated to No 527 Sqn. But the days of flak, fire and counter-fire were over. For this ageing *Spitfire* (in operational terms) the war was over. Her new unit had been formed to carry out the rather sedate but necessary task of radar calibration. The Squadron's equipment consisted of a mix of battle-weary *Blenheims, Hurricane Mk Is,* and *Spitfire Mk Vs*.

In any event, *AB910s* RAF service was all but over. She remained with the unit for a further year, doubtless adding a little spice to a mundane job. On 30th May, 1946, the venerable fighter was delivered to a maintenance unit to await her fate.

For a *Spitfire Mk V,* born in August, 1941, the sands of time were fast running out. 'Fate' could logically mean only one thing—the scrapyard. An aircraft, after all, is by itself an inanimate object, much as we like to think otherwise. When its useful life is over it is only sensible to make it into saucepans just as saucepans were once made into aircraft. (They were not, in fact, but let us not spoil the myth).

But occasionally, fate takes a different turn. For *AB910,* salvation materialised in the shape of the late Air Commodore Allen Wheeler, an aviator of long and honourable standing. After six long years of war in Europe, Allen decided to turn his hand to a little sports flying. Casting around for a suitable mount, he took a fancy to *AB910,* and took it out of the hands of the RAF on 14th July, 1947. He stripped her of her roundels, abandoned her service number (as did so many of her human counterparts), provided her with a Certificate of Airworthiness and registered her as *G-AISU*.

"Fine feathers make fine birds", so it is said. For the next few years *SU* appeared here and there, usually as a participant in air racing, in a fetching blue colour scheme.

Allen Wheeler's ownership turned out to be a long-term good omen for the ten-year-old fighter. In the early '50s she returned to her makers, Vickers-Armstrongs Ltd., who completely renovated her, re-dressed her in respectable camouflage, and replaced her original RAF serial number, *AB910*. She was then given the squadron code letters, *QJ-J*—which was not strictly accurate historically, as the aircraft had never flown with 92 Sqn or 616 Sqn, both of which wore the code *QJ* at one time or another. The choice of letters, widely taken to be a well-deserved accolade to Chief Development Test Pilot Jeffrey Quill OBE AFC from the *Spitfire* prototype days of 1936, was, in fact, an arbitrary choice based on the record of No 92 Sqn as the highest scoring fighter squadron, and the individual letter J because that aircraft had been flown by three of 92 Sqn's wartime commanders—Jamie Rankin, Johnnie Kent and Neville Duke. As things turned out, it was Jeffrey Quill who was to do much of the latter day flying in *AB910* during its last days with Vickers-Armstrongs. He flew it on numerous occasions at various air displays for the next twelve years.

Spitfires Reborn

Appropriately, it was Jeffrey Quill who, on 15th September 1965, climbed into *AB910* for the last time to deliver the *Spitfire* back to the RAF—to the Battle of Britain Flight, which was still based at RAF Coltishall. It was to be that noted test pilot's last *Spitfire* flight. In his book *"Spitfire*—A Test Pilot's Story", he tells of his sadness in 'bidding farewell to an old and trusted friend'.

As for *AB910*, she had been delivered into good hands. After a long and chequered career as a wartime fighter, a radar 'stooge', a civilian racer, a company PR and display aircraft, *AB910* had, after a quarter of a century returned to her former masters to begin a new career. She is with them yet.

Another remarkable survivor is an even earlier *Spitfire* to come off the production line at Castle Bromwich, a *Mk IIA, P7350*. (It should be explained that, for some curious reason, the RAF at one time insisted on using Roman numerals, so the mark number indicates two rather than eleven). This aircraft is the oldest flyable *Spitfire* serving with the Flight, having emerged from the factory some 51 years ago as the 14th off the line. She was to be followed by a further 11,925 *Spitfires* from that same source.

Her first operational unit was No 266 (Rhodesia) Sqn. at RAF Wittering, near Peterborough, where she arrived on 6th September, 1940. There followed the usual bewildering moves from pillar to post so typical of wartime aircraft. After just one month with 266 Sqn. P7350 was transferred to the renowned 603 (City of Edinburgh) Sqn. of the Royal Auxiliary Air Force (RAuxAF). Within days she sustained quite serious damage when her pilot, Pilot Officer Martel, carried out a forced landing after a combat involving a *Me bf109* over Hastings. After repairs had been completed, *P7350* was allocated to another Auxiliary squadron, No 616, based at Tangmere near Chichester. Scarcely had the paint of her new code letters dried when she was passed on to 64 Sqn. at Hornchurch on 10th April, 1941, just prior to that unit's move to Turnhouse, Scotland.

By that time, front-line squadrons were being re-equipped with *Spitfire Mk Vs*. That was probably the case with 64 Sqn. as, by 5th August 1941, *P7350's* short and turbulent operational life was over. After another overhaul followed by several month's storage she joined the strength of Central Gunnery School which was based at Sutton Bridge, near Spalding, Lincolnshire.

But not for long. After another accident on 4th February, 1943, *P7350* was sent to Hamble, Hampshire, for repair, went to 57 Operational Training Unit on 20th March, suffered another accident one month later, was returned to Hamble and, after repair, consigned to storage at Colerne, near Chippenham, Wiltshire.

There she remained. The months and years passed her by while she stood, silent and unwanted. Some five years later, after a post-war clear-out, *P7350* went under the auctioneer's hammer. She was sold to John Dale Ltd., scrap merchants, for the paltry sum of twenty-five pounds, an amount which would not even buy her clock today. Indeed, if she were offered for sale — and she won't be — something in the region of three-quarters of a million pounds would change hands.

How, then, did that veteran escape the fate which was apparently upon her?

By the greatest of good fortune, when she was taken away by her new owners, her log-books went with her. Someone browsed through them, having nothing better to do at the time, and recognised the *Spitfire's* historic importance. By co-incidence, whilst one part of RAF Colerne was busily clearing its hangars and selling serviceable, historic aircraft for scrap at knock-down prices, another part of the same station had started to utilise vacant hangar space by setting up a museum. The directors of John Dale Ltd. must have known about this, for the company generously donated their twenty-five pounds worth of veteran aircraft back to RAF Colerne where she was added to the collection.

So time passed until, some twenty years later, in a nationwide search for aircraft to take part in the film "The Battle of Britain" (about which more later) *P7350* came under scrutiny. Despite the passage of so much time, she had been kept in a controlled environment, and was found to be in excellent order. The old aircraft was given a thorough overhaul before once again taking to the air on her delivery flight to RAF Duxford, on 20th May, 1968 — twenty-four years after her previous sortie. She was flown by Flt Lt 'Nobby' Armstrong who, like the aircraft, had been loaned to the film unit, *Spitfire* Productions Ltd..

Spitfires Reborn

Although the *Spitfire* was painted in the correct camouflage appropriate to 1940, she was given a civilian registration, *G-AWIJ*. *P7350* (as we will continue to call her) played a prominent part in that epic film. She even carried out some flying in France when bad weather interfered with the schedule in England. On completion of her contract as a film star *P7350* was returned to the RAF. This time there was no question about her fate. She was allocated to the Battle of Britain Flight, and on 6th November 1968 she was delivered to RAF Coltishall by Sqn Ldr Tim Mills. She has flown with the BBF ever since.

The Battle of Britain Memorial Flight—The People

In 1972 the Hawker Aircraft Co. made a most generous gesture. Realising the importance of the Battle of Britain Flight, and its mission to preserve for posterity flying examples of the nation's history, the Company decided to present the RAF with the last *Hurricane* to leave the production line. *Hawker Hurricane Mk II PZ865* joined the Flight in 1972. One year later *Avro Lancaster B1 PA474*, having been restored to flying condition by No 44 Squadron, was added to the fleet.

The unit, by that time firmly established within both the Service and the hearts of the people, now formally became The Battle of Britain Memorial Flight with its own crest bearing the motto, Lest We Forget. It made another move to RAF Coningsby, Lincolnshire, in 1976. where it has been comfortably ensconced ever since. The days of scuttling from one lodging place to another, as base after base was closed, the constant financial scrutinies, and the nail-biting, unremitting uncertainty over the Flight's future—or possibly, lack of it—are now part of the unit's history.

With the willing co-operation of North Kesteven District Council it has even become a tourist attraction as part of the increasingly popular Airfield Trail. The BBMF has, as another old war-horse once said in a different context, 'moved into the sunlit uplands' of universal acceptance and widespread support.

Who makes it work? And how is it done?

The Battle of Britain Memorial Flight

To the surprise of many, including a number of Service people who should know better, there is only one established officer post — the Flight's Commanding Officer. He is the senior manager, administrator and general overseer of everything involved in the running of a unique unit consisting of seven types of aircraft, all in flying condition, the 'stars' publicly demonstrated under stringent safety and preservation rules. He is also, almost by-the-way, the one and only captain of the *Lancaster*.

All the other aircrew who spend many week-ends of the year demonstrating the priceless fleet are volunteers, either from the *Tornado* force which shares RAF Coningsby with the Flight, or from further afield in the case of the navigators and flight engineers who help to crew the *Lancaster*.

Until his selection to take up this singular and demanding job, Squadron Leader Colin Paterson had followed a quite normal RAF career with a maritime reconnaissance background flying *Shackletons* and *Nimrods* from the United Kingdom, Malta and Gibraltar. He had also done a stint as a qualified flying instructor, plus a couple of staff appointments thrown in for good measure. He had entered the RAF through its College at Cranwell, Near, Lincolnshire, in 1957, and has been in charge of the BBMF for almost three years.

"I didn't exactly seek the job," says Colin. "It came out of the blue during one of my regular career interviews. It looked at the time as though I would again be destined for a desk job, as I had already completed one flying job in the rank. The opportunity to take over the Flight came almost as an afterthought in the minds of the personnel people. It was most probably my *Shackleton* experience which gave them the idea."

The *Shackleton*, of course, is a direct descendant of the *Lancaster*, and is the last of the four-engined heavy piston-powered aircraft left in the RAF, and will shortly be retired from its task in the airborne early warning role in favour of the new AWACS currently entering service.

Like most aircrew, Colin is always ready to talk about his job, but not so ready to talk about himself. That is as it should be. One of the essential ingredients of his task is that he must exercise an unobtrusive sense of diplomacy at all times. The successful achievement of the Flight's mission is entirely dependant upon the voluntary

Spitfires Reborn

services of aircrews who are already very much absorbed in their daily round, which is highly demanding and concerned with very different 'state of the art' aircraft and their highly technical systems. Most of them are family men with a wife and children to be considered, and all the domestic chores and responsibilities which that happy state brings in its train.

Another consideration is that, although Colin has a very real job as C.O. of the Flight, the aircrews upon whom he relies so heavily are, in effect, 'borrowed'. Their first loyalty must rest with their own units and senior officers. Of course, every serving man and woman in the Royal Air Force is immensely proud of the BBMF and the noble heritage it represents, and it is certain that the closer they are to the Flight the more understanding and supportive they are. It is also true to say that the fascination – and the imposed trust – connected with flying those survivors of another age is in itself self-motivating. Nevertheless, those volunteers, fully stretched as they are by their primary duties, must take on the extra training and background studies required. Also, they and their families must face the facts of more absences from home, mainly when everyone else is off duty during the summertime. These extra burdens are willingly accepted for no return other than the sheer pride and exhilaration they engender. That is a personal commitment of the highest order.

Is there, then, any difficulty in finding sufficient volunteers?

"We need five pilots, maybe six at the outside where the fighters are concerned," says Colin. "Although we rarely have pilots queuing up to join us, we really have no trouble in finding that number. We don't need to look further afield than our own home here at Coningsby, and that is very convenient. Given the many hours of overtime we ask of our pilots it is essential that full advantage is taken of the time they can spare from their off-duty periods."

Within the BBMF's headquarters, with its suite of busy offices, lecture room and crewroom, there is an air of quiet dedication. One gets the firm impression that everyone there feels a sense of privilege and responsibility. The aircrews are a far cry from the hard-drinking, vociferous caricatures as frequently imagined by the layman and so often depicted on the screen and in fiction. The expression 'ace' is rarely heard, except in banter, in the RAF in general, and never in the Battle of Britain Memorial Flight.

Squadron Leader Paul Day, professional fighter pilot to his finger-tips and holder of the Air Force Cross, epitomises the quiet air of enthusiasm one finds throughout the Flight. As befits one whose daily bread-and-butter is earned at the sharp end of the nation's most advanced military aircraft, the so-called variable geometry, or 'swing-wing' Mach 2 *Tornado*, Paul is one who deals in facts rather than fantasy. Self-delusion is unknown to him.

Unusually, he came into the business of military aviation almost by default. "I don't recall ever having any burning desire to fly when I was younger," he said. It seems that he first sought a 'proper job' in industry as a management trainee in road haulage and bulk storage with a multi-national oil company.

"I really tried hard," he went on, "but I found it all so utterly boring. In the end I fell for the RAF's act, and I've been hooked on it ever since"

So Paul turned his back on the security of commerce and threw in his lot with other like-minded youngsters who set off in a different direction in 1961 to enter what was to become an exciting career in military aviation. Paul was one of the first 'all-through' jet trainees as pioneered by the RAF. It was the beginning of an era when youngsters would take their very first instructional flight in a pure-jet aircraft (aptly named the *Jet Provost*), and come out at the far end of the training pipeline complete with wings and an RAF officer's commission without ever having seen a propeller. In so doing, Paul fell victim to the early teething troubles of the diminutive *Gnat* trainer, which meant that he found himself undergoing his advanced training in the ageing *Vampire T.11* trainer. He thoroughly enjoyed the experience which, he learned as had many others before him, that lessons from a more primitive—and also, perhaps demanding— aircraft can often make for better learning where basic aeronautical truths are concerned.

There were now no doubts as to the direction in which Paul's life would go. After the *Vampire* he went to Chivenor, Devon, to carry out operational conversion to the *Hawker Hunter* which Paul described as "...the *jet-Spitfire*, the last of the sports models." He went

Spitfires Reborn

on to fly that sleek and beautiful aircraft for a further 2,000 hours in the Far East, Middle East and the United Kingdom.

With such a thorough and enjoyable grounding in the exclusive world of fighter flying, it is hardly surprising that Paul Day needed to tread very delicately to avoid the twin traps which lie in wait for many who decide to follow a career in the Service. On the one hand, having earned one's spurs, there is the path which follows the beckoning finger of ambition to achieve high rank, greater power — and next to no flying. On the other hand there is flying to be had, of a kind, but at the cost of career and excitement. Worthy and necessary flying, it is true, and better than none at all. Communications, 'stooging' for guns and radars, radio calibration and the like. But for a young man who turned away from boredom for the adventure of military flying it was necessary to tread the narrow path between stardom and the prosaic.

Paul Day has achieved that feat with undeniable success. He has managed to pursue a life of constant, front-line flying since those earlier *Hunter* days. He passed on to the *McDonnell F4 Phantom* for a further 3,000 hours. During that period of his life Paul experienced yet another aspect of the flying life. He carried out a thoroughly enjoyable, yet exhilarating, tour as an Exchange Officer with the US Air Force. He served as Flight Commander with two USAF squadrons based in Arizona — situations which engendered mutual respect.

After the American experience Paul returned to Coningsby, still with *Phantoms*. That superb aircraft had become truly multi-role in most respects — just as the *Spitfire* had done many years before. The *F4's* capabilities, of course, were by this time in a totally different league due to the immense advances in technology in every direction — engine, weaponry, navigation and attack systems, photography, et al.

The Day family quickly settled down to life again at Coningsby. The daily round kept him as busy and interested as ever. His off-duty hours, with all the domestic concerns which go with a growing family, were fully occupied. It is hardly surprising that, up to that point, he had never seriously considered trying to squeeze in yet another commitment as extensive as volunteering his services to the Battle of Britain Memorial Flight.

Not until, that is, the then Station Commander drew him aside one evening at some social occasion in the Mess to make a fairly positive suggestion that it would be to the advantage of all concerned if he were to become actively embroiled with the BBMF. Although, let it be understood, no pressure was being applied from on high, it is always prudent to pay due regard to opinions from such a source. The result was that Paul Day did, indeed, offer his services to the Flight in 1979.

As is usually the case, he spent the two ensuing seasons in getting to know the *Hurricane*. That was a far cry from the *Phantom* flying of everyday life. Paul quickly realised that this fighter of fifty years ago, with its design and imposed restrictions, had much to teach him about the flying business despite his already lengthy experience.

He recalled his first encounter clearly. "I soon realised," he said, "that everything that is second nature to today's fast jet pilot is often quite inappropriate to a big piston. For instance, the cockpit environment of both *Spitfires* and *Hurricanes*, judged by today's standards, is unbelievably primitive. The pilot is subject to engine noise, exhaust fumes, howling draughts and rattles. Instruments and ancillary controls are often awkwardly positioned, and visibility from the cockpit—even with the reflector gunsight removed—is a constant flight safety hazard."

"During that first *Hurricane* trip," Paul recalled, "I was happily cruising around, getting the feel of things, when I though it would be a good idea to try a 'twinkle' roll. Well, it wasn't. In next to no time I found myself still inverted at 2,000 feet of so, going rapidly downwards at forty-five degrees towards Mother Earth." It was clear from the telling that the memory had a salutary effect. "It never happened again," Paul concluded ruefully.

And so season followed season. Paul Day has now flown with the BBMF for eleven years. In the meantime, his children have grown into adulthood. Paul moved on from his beloved *Phantom* to the *Tornado*, at one end of the flying spectrum, and to the *Spitfires* at the other. He has now gathered almost 1,000 hard-won hours on the vintage fighters, including some time put in on behalf of some civilian owners. He has demonstrated the grace and romance of the last of the piston-engined warplanes on countless occasions before millions of spectators. He has also become the Flight's Fighter Leader in

Spitfires Reborn

whose competent hands the training of other volunteer pilots rests. As yet another season approaches, with its week-ends away and constant extra-curricular activity, does he not occasionally wonder what sort of masochism has overtaken him?

"Not really," says this quiet, good-humoured man who once claimed 'no burning ambition' to fly. "There is always a new pilot to work up — and flying high-performance vintage pistons never comes easily to a jet pilot. They have to learn that our primary concern is to maintain these aircraft, for the nation and the RAF, in flying condition for as long as we can. We must treat them with due care and attention. Display flying, in the normally accepted sense, is a secondary consideration."

Finally, but most importantly, doesn't all this extra work and responsibility create unwanted stress at home?

"One must definitely have an understanding wife," says Paul. "I've always been fortunate in that respect. My wife has accepted the fact that I've yet to find out what I want to do when I grow up!"

Lightly said, with 'an economy of the truth'. This man, one instinctively feels, knows exactly what he is doing, and why. We are a fortunate people indeed — and always have been — to find that sort of dedication to the nation's heritage amongst us. But Squadron Leader Paul Day would never admit to that.

Far from the swarms of jostling aircraft buffs and the frenzied activities of the air pageants, the BBMF hangar at Coningsby in mid-winter presents an atmosphere of cloistral calm. With the great end doors closed against the dust whipped up by an icy east wind, and the shriek of *Tornado* after-burners, there is a surgery-like air about the place. The spotless floor glistens like a lake.

The *Hurricanes* and *Spitfires*, partially dismembered stand silent beside the work-benches and tool racks in their allotted bays.

At one end of the hangar the *Avro Lancaster* bomber presides over the scene. At least, most of it does for it, too, has various parts of its anatomy removed to enable the detailed winter inspection to be carried out.

This is the domain of the eighteen established ground crews who cosset their charges with such care. Led by Warrant Officer Barry Sears, the engine and airframe fitters, electricians, instrument and

The Battle of Britain Memorial Flight

The BBMF hanger at Coningsby, with the aeroplanes undergoing winter conservation and maintenance ready for the summer season that lies ahead.

radio men have learnt the technical intricacies of these old, complicated and sometimes cumbersome charges through 'on-the-job' training. Formal lecture-room instruction is virtually a thing of the past where these long obsolete aircraft are concerned. With the help of a reasonably comprehensive library of surviving publications these young airmen, basically trained in the methods and technologies of a much later era, learn the skills required by painstakingly practical application on the shop floor.

As one would expect, planned maintenance of RAF aircraft has undergone vast changes with the passing years. The introduction of jet power, with its greatly improved reliability compared with the latter-day powerful piston, has brought about radical changes in servicing practises. Modular exchange of components and improved technical recording and logistic support made possible by today's computers are just two of the many factors which have added to the widening gulf separating today's maintenance requirements from those of World War 2.

Fifty years ago all RAF aircraft were treated to a Daily Inspection (DI) every twenty-four hours, periodic minor servicings at squadron level, and major servicings in the workshops every 180 flying hours (if they lasted that long). Such a cycle would be unnecessarily intensive of effort and manpower for the aircraft operated by the BBMF, despite their years. That is because of their low utilisation rate, the individual care and attention devoted to each aircraft of the small fleet and, most significantly, the carefully restricted manner in which the aircraft are flown. In the interests of preservation their days of 'flat out or bust' are long gone. Today, the top speed of the fighters never exceeds a stately 275 knots, negative 'G' is avoided, positive manoeuvres never go beyond +3G, and flight through heavy precipitation (rain, hail, etc.) is taboo. Consequently, the Flight's fighters now undergo major servicing after 360 flying hours, or every six years, whichever the sooner. Lesser servicings take place every 60 hours or annually.

With strict adherence to these rules of preservation, Barry Sears estimates that the aircraft will be able to continue to delight their fans until well into the 21st Century.

The passage of the years has, of course, resulted in a vast reduction in the ready supply of spare parts. All possible sources have been tapped, from the robbing of the gate guardians to the bits and pieces squirrelled away by individuals in attics and garages. In the latter case, the range of items so preserved is astonishing. Tail and main wheels, rear view mirrors, flight and engine instruments emerge from dusty recesses from time to time, and are donated to the Flight.

As is the case in time of war, improvisation frequently plays a part. The *Devon's* brake linings have been adapted for use in the *Spitfire XIX*; bits of the *Hawker Hunter's* pneumatic system have been fitted to the *Hurricanes*; instruments and electrical components can often be interchanged between different aircraft types. Service workshops can sometimes be prevailed upon to manufacture parts where suitable drawings and specifications exist. As a last resort, spares may be sought from the growing number of specialist dealers, but this is avoided whenever possible as such people are not noted for their magnanimity.

The most dramatic example of the lengths taken to 'keep 'em flying' concerns the three *Griffon*-engined *Spitfires*. In the early '70s it was clear that the need to find a replacement for the *Griffons* was of paramount importance if the *Mk XIXs* were to remain flyable. The most likely source of supply seemed to be the engines which would become available upon the impending demise of the *Shackleton* maritime reconnaissance fleet.

"That was not as straightforward as it might seem," reports Barry Sears. "The *Shackleton* used contra-rotating airscrews which require complicated gearing between the engine and the propellers. Also, the casing of the supercharger is three-quarters of an inch wider than the original, and could not be fitted into the existing engine bearers. There were at least twenty or so other snags to overcome."

The co-operation over a number of years by Rolls Royce, British Aerospace and the Battle of Britain Memorial Flight enabled the necessary adaptations to be made. The first Rolls Royce *Griffon 58* to be fitted into a *Spitfire* took to the air in *Spitfire XIX PS915* in December, 1986, followed by *PS853* in August 1989.

"They are hybrids, of course," says Barry, "but they are aesthetically viable. With any luck they might still be around for the *Spitfire's* centenary celebrations in 2036!"

The same sense of dedicated enthusiasm exhibited by the Flight's volunteer aircrews is shared by the eighteen technical tradesmen on the posted strength. They, also, are volunteers in the sense that the appeal of embracing the unique skills involved in working with vintage aircraft led them to seek employment with the BBMF.

Corporal Bob Mitchell is an engine fitter who joined the Flight in 1984. Previously he had worked principally with *Hunter* aircraft at RAF Abingdon. It was certainly work that he had enjoyed, but the lure of veteran aircraft drew him to RAF Coningsby. Whether it is a sense of pride engendered by the historic nature of the Flight, or an engineer's fascination with the unusual challenges associated with the successful operation of old machines, is hard to say. Bob Mitchell's own word for the attraction is 'romantic', and he is quite certain that the seven years he has spent with the BBMF have been the happiest of his life in the RAF.

There are disadvantages, of course. Bob's contemporaries in the wider world beyond this cocoon of preserved history can more readily keep abreast of constantly advancing methods and technology; The unit itself is a small one, seen by some to be locked in a time warp; all of which inhibits an individual's chances in the promotion competition.

"It's all worthwhile, though," says Bob, "just for the pleasure of working with these wonderful aircraft. Also, there's a lot to be said for the stability my wife and I have had since we came to Coningsby. It's true that there's a lot of week-end work during the season, but we haven't had to pack up our home to move every two or three years on posting."

Bob Mitchell is an airframe fitter and supervisor. As such, he is qualified to work on all the aircraft types operated by the unit. In one or two respects that has meant learning new (or, perhaps, old) tricks of the trade. The most obvious one is working with fabric, as with the *Hurricanes* and some control surfaces on the other aircraft. Also, in an age of 'fly by wire' and powered control systems, working with the BBMF fleet means turning the clock back to pilot-operated wires and rods.

The technical reference books are skimpy by today's standards. This is compensated for by the wealth of practical experience built up over the years. The BBMF sees itself as the custodian of the

The Battle of Britain Memorial Flight

highest standards of workmanship, and its expertise is readily available to civilian owners and operators in similar fields—although the demand for such consultancy services is less sought after these days as the vintage aircraft movement develops.

Bob, like his Commanding Officer, is probably approaching his final season with the BBMF. One senses that he views the prospect with mixed feelings. On the one hand, there is a great big world out there—the 'real' world—where a good man can move up the ladder of promotion. On the other hand, Bob will have to leave behind him these precious survivors of a bygone age, all of which he has grown to know so well over the years.

Whatever the future holds for him Bob knows that he has been privileged to play a key role in linking today's Royal Air Force and, indeed, the British people, with what was aptly described as the nation's finest hour.

A BBMF Spitfire is rolled out after it's winter resoration—an event that always creates considerable interest with the ground crew, who can be seen in the background.

Spitfires Reborn

The short winter's day draws to a damp and chilly close. The mists begin to settle over the flat lands of Lincolnshire. Occasionally, the crackle of a *Tornado*'s after-burner echoes through the buildings and roads of the base as its lurid mauve trail disappears into the gloom beyond Tattershall Keep.

As today's young aviators take their places at the very forefront of military technology, the few survivors of the bitter aerial battles of half a century ago stand silently by as their minders and menders pack away their tools and don their jackets. Another day of 'TLC' (a Barry Sears' expression meaning 'tender, loving care') is over.

The departing visitor expresses his farewells and thanks. The lights of RAF Coningsby fade rapidly away in the enveloping mists. It is natural then to feel just a little of the pride and satisfaction shared by those whose work reminds us, year after year, of the courage and sacrifices of another generation of a bygone era. It is all so aptly summarised in the motto of the Battle of Britain Memorial Flight: "Lest we Forget".

CHAPTER TWO

A Bonny, Wee Scot

Group Captain T C Mahaddie DSO DFC AFC, holder of the Czech Military Cross, qualified pilot and engineer was, as he will proudly tell you, a 'bomber baron'. More explicitly, he flew *Whitley* and *Stirling* bombers through the deadly night skies over Germany during that period when the RAF's Bomber Command represented the only effective way in which the war could be carried to the enemy. In 1943 he was selected to become a founder member of Air Vice-Marshal Don Bennett's famed Pathfinder Force.

But that is a dramatic story of sustained bravery in its own right. What, then, is that distinguished airman's connection with our theme concerning the rescue and preservation of *Spitfire* fighter aircraft?

Hamish Mahaddie — for that is the name by which he has been known for more years than anyone can remember — is here because it so happened that, at one significant time, he became the catalyst that provided the impetus which led in time to the veteran aircraft preservation industry as we know it today. In particular, although he may not have fully realised the consequences of his activities at the time, it was he who garnered the rusting hulks of many of the *Spitfires* we so much enjoy seeing today.

Hamish, although a fully qualified engineer, did not don his overalls to strip down near-wrecks, cut metal and rivet everything back into place. His task was, in a way, more fundamental than that. He

Spitfires Reborn

was given the responsibility, against a tight deadline and budget, to track down as many World War 2 fighters, British and German, as he could find. Plus, as time went on, German bombers and transport aircraft.

We will look back to that significant time, 1965-67, to find out why and how it all happened. But as a prelude to this part of our story let us get to know its subject a little better.

Hamish Mahaddie is, of course, a wee Scot. That is immediately discernable from his diminutive stature and his rich, lyrical brogue. He made his first, small impact in this world on 19th March, 1911, the son of an unemployed house painter and a partially crippled mother. Times were indeed hard.

Three years later the catastrophe of the Kaiser's War broke out, and on that very day Tam Mahaddie took himself off as a proud Gordon Highlander in defence of his King and country. Hamish can still remember certain sights and sounds of the years which followed. His father's home leaves, the awesome cigar-shape of a *Zeppelin,* the bombing of a bonded whisky warehouse in Leith Docks, leading to unconfirmed reports that some of the liquid gold was saved in milk bottles and jam jars as it ran down the gutters.

After a brief and very basic schooling Hamish left, at the age of thirteen years, to earn his fortune in a nearby grocer's shop, there to become a filler of wine and beer bottles. Apparently, that early start in the world of commerce left him unimpressed, for in January, 1928, he surprised himself and others by passing the entrance examination for the RAF's Trenchard Experiment (the boys' technical training scheme) at RAF Halton, near Aylesbury, Buckinghamshire. He donned RAF blue for the first time to take his place with the 17th Entry of aircraft apprentices.

Eventually, after much burning of the midnight oil, Leading Aircraftsman Hamish Mahaddie passed out as a fully qualified metal rigger. He packed his kit-bag and made his way to Lincolnshire to join that other shining symbol of the Trenchardian era, the RAF College, Cranwell, Lincolnshire. There, he was able to consolidate his training in the workshops, servicing old *Avro 504s, Siskins* and *Audaxes.* There were plenty of sporting opportunities, also, which enabled him to add tennis to his already lengthy list of activities.

In his 20th year Hamish, by now a confident, practical engineer, turned his back on the flat, bleak fields of Lincolnshire to board the legendary troopship *Somersetshire*, a vessel so pristine, as we are reminded in RAF folk-song, that '...the skipper looked on her with pride'. Indeed, 'he'd have a blue fit' if he saw any sh**t on the side of his lovely vessel.'

During the lengthy voyage south Hamish and his fellow travellers bedecked themselves in khaki drill uniform and donned their Bombay Bowlers (sun helmets). The ship eventually deposited its human cargo at Basra where they were dispersed to a variety of bases. Hamish finally found himself at Hinaidi, Mesopotamia ('Mespot' then, Iraq today).

There, he plied his trade as a rigger with No 70 Squadron. Whether it was his technical expertise, or his prowess at tennis, or perhaps both, he certainly made his mark. His seniors recommended that he undertake pilot training. So off he went to Egypt to earn his wings.

Having done so, Sergeant Mahaddie returned to Mespot to complete his lengthy overseas tour. In 1937, just in time for the beginnings of rearmament and the war, he arrived back in the United Kingdom.

The Mahaddie story of World War 2 is exciting, touching, and wholly honourable. It is too full of incident to repeat here; it would also suffer by being out of context. It is well recounted in his own book, "HAMISH" — required reading for all who wish to learn, through one man's personal experiences, more about the first fifty years of the world's first independent air force.

Suffice it to say now that the war came to an end in its own good time, after six long years. The boy apprentice engineer of 1928 had learned and risked much, endured peaks and troughs of joy and sadness; and he was now a highly decorated and respected pilot and senior officer.

Hamish continued to serve in the Royal Air Force into the so-called 'peacetime' years, although they were often anything but that. Reading between the lines of his memoirs one gets a strong impression that post-war service was very much of an anti-climax for him. After commanding a transport wing in Germany for a while, he was selected to attend Staff College in Haifa, Palestine (as it then was).

Spitfires Reborn

It was a move which created dissatisfaction to all concerned, himself included.

The high spot thereafter seems to have been the England to New Zealand Air Race of 1953 which Hamish helped to plan. Once that piece of excitement had faded into history nothing much seems to have happened until he donned his bowler hat on 24th March, 1958, and walked away from the service he had joined thirty years before.

So where was the fighter connection? How did the 'bomber baron' from way back have any influence on today's thriving historic aircraft industry? I decided to call on him to find out.

The small but still sprightly figure led the way through the quiet, pleasant house a stone's throw away from the seashore at Pagham, West Sussex. I had met Hamish on one or two occasions before, and had found our casual relationship to be friendly and easy-going. As I followed him along the corridor I wondered, not for the first time, how this small figure managed to cope for hours on end with the mighty *Stirling* bomber.

We arrived at his study door. The room was lined to the ceiling with shelves; every conceivable book on military aviation seemed to be there. The few wall spaces between contained framed photos and personal memorabilia. By way of furniture there was a desk and study chair, an easy chair, and a made-up bed. A cupboard door was slightly ajar providing a tantalising glimpse of the odd bottle containing some amber fluid.

There was a familiar ambience about it all, which at first I could not quite identify. Then it dawned on me. We were seated in a room which could easily have been a single officer's quarter in any Officers' Mess of the RAF. I felt at home and thoroughly relaxed. So we started to talk about how it was that a bomber baron had been instrumental in bringing old fighters back to life.

The boy who had needed to cram before he could take the entrance exam at Halton, like many of us, had to cram at virtually every successive stepping-stone of his life in the service. Particularly in the flying business. Unlike doctors, parsons, school-teachers, and many other professions, who seem to be able to gain a passport to a livelihood which can absolve them from undertaking any further great tests of their professionalism, RAF aircrew are never permitted to freewheel. Their own lives, at the very least, depend upon their skills and knowledge being maintained at a peak. Those who fly with them in whatever capacity place implicit trust in their ability to see them safely back on the ground. So, where RAF flying is concerned, the powers-that-be make very sure that, firstly, skill's are kept sharp despite the passage of time and, secondly, operational aircrews are mentally and academically capable of matching up to the constant technological advances which are part of military aviation. So, it is cram, cram, cram all the way.

Each one of us knew that the time would come, one day, when one or other of the traps would indicate that one's performance had peaked — that, regardless of effort, no further acceleration would be possible. (Each one, that is, except one, and he becomes Chief of the Air Staff). It is a time when one finds oneself struggling ever harder to stay in the same place.

The moment of truth for Hamish came, I believe, in 1947 at the Haifa Staff College. It was, for him, a wholly new ball-game. His long service life had been spent in a spirit of mutual trust and assistance. One's fellows, recognising the need for a helping hand to be extended whenever a flying colleague looked like foundering beneath the weight of pure theory, always did their utmost to help.

Staff College is different — a watershed. It is (or was then) the last gateway to very senior rank, influence and power. It was also the place which rang warning bells that flying days are finite, and that a lengthy future of pen-pushing and conferences might lie ahead.

Also, by 1947, the older veterans, such as Hamish who had already served nineteen exacting years, were finding that some of the young tigers with whom they had to pit their wits were long on learning and short on mutual co-operation. For them the glittering prizes of promotion and power were too important to squander time and effort on others. As Hamish succinctly remarked: "One was left entirely to one's own devices, and I never recovered from that initial shock..."

What he did not realise at the time, but came to appreciate later, was that many of the doctrinal lessons he had tried to absorb at Haifa would stand him in good stead in later life.

As we have seen, Hamish Mahaddie retired from active service with the Royal Air Force on 24th March, 1958, after tucking thirty years of brave and honourable service into his sporran.

Spitfires Reborn

Most regular service people face an uncertain future at that point, with the possible exception of the most senior air marshals who always seem to have something fairly lucrative and prestigious awaiting them — a few directorships, or a ceremonial State appointment — something that will enable them to keep up appearances before other Knights of the Realm. For the majority, the difficulty is that they retire at a relatively young age (usually fifty-five at the latest), are more or less impecunious (no-one gets rich on service pay), and they are forced to try to cut in to a labour market which, in their age bracket, is already over-subscribed.

Some take on mundane time-serving appointments at the Ministry of Defence or some other Government department. Others receive a pittance administering charities. Some go independent and broke at the same time. A few become successful consultants.

There are two essentials when embarking on the latter course. First, get hold of a good printer who can design and produce a tasteful business card. Second, one must know at least a few people in influential positions who might at least read your card before consigning it to the paper bin.

If, by chance, one emerges from the Service having found a niche in the memory banks of the mighty (in the nicest possible way), things can take a distinct upward turn. Such is likely to be the case if one is a small, sprightly Scot, sports a name like Hamish, possesses a lyrical accent which encourages all to think that one is canny, and has notched up a record of long and loyal service in war and peace.

Whilst on retirement leave, Hamish became aware that there were, indeed, one or two important people ready to relieve themselves of certain onerous aspects of their affairs, and thought that he was the very chap to handle them. Thus, he found himself unwittingly taking on an instant consultancy, and the means to operate it from a plush office near Park Lane, assisted by a pleasing young Girl Friday.

One day, somewhat to his surprise, Hamish was offered the job of Technical Adviser for a film (he, being in the business, calls them 'movies'). It was to be entitled '633 Squadron'. It was concerned with *Mosquito* aircraft — so who better? The film was made, and was much enjoyed by audiences everywhere. More importantly, it made a handsome profit.

A Bonny, Wee Scot

That film paved the way for Hamish to play a part in the making of a total of fifteen feature films. These included 'Operation Crossbow', 'General Patton' and at least a couple of James Bond epics. Although one assumes they were all qualified successes artistically or at the box office, or both, there were some from which Hamish distances himself as being historically inaccurate. A man of principle, he even disclaimed a credit rating in the case of 'A Bridge Too Far' which, although a resounding box-office success, he felt that "...history had been treated in an extremely lax fashion."

The successful penetration by Hamish of the strange, eccentric business of film-making eventually led to the one-time bomber baron meeting the world of the fighter boys.

The epic picture 'Battle of Britain' was originally the brainchild of one who had become a big name in the British film industry, active and flourishing as it was in those days. His name was Ben Fisz. He was a large, good-humoured Pole who had arrived in England during the war to become a *Hurricane* and *Spitfire* pilot.

It was Ben Fisz who first floated the idea that it might still be possible to produce an historically accurate film, using a fictional but believable story line, against the background of the Battle of Britain. From the outset, he stipulated that the picture must achieve realism by the use of colour and wide screen techniques. Clearly, that precluded the use of archive film on both counts. Fisz also came down firmly against the use of models, however brilliantly they had been constructed. As every aviation enthusiast knows only too well, such devices are instantly detectable, and give an air of unreality.

The proviso, that real aircraft only could be used for the picture's air and ground sequences seemed, in 1965, to raise an insurmountable obstacle. Had not the Ministry of Defence just spent years selling off thousands of prematurely retired aircraft for a handful of silver? Furthermore, if it was seemingly impossible to beg, borrow or steal British aircraft twenty-six years after the event, where on earth was the 'enemy' to be found?

Ben Fisz's brainchild was almost killed off at birth. But he was not the man to surrender without a struggle. He had managed to interest influential people in the idea of the film. But that was about

Spitfires Reborn

all. So far, there was nothing tangible in sight. Everything, in 1966, existed only in Ben Fisz's fertile mind.

He was, nevertheless, sufficiently persuasive to induce the renowned film-maker Harry Salzmann to throw in his lot with him in May, 1966. From that moment, by combined effort, things started to move forward. Both Fisz and Salzmann were men who made things happen.

Despite the strong combination of personalities the months dragged on as proposals, counter-proposals, ideas, wrangles and disappointments followed one upon the other. But that is a story in its own right, interestingly told in Leonard Moseley's book, 'The Battle of Britain – The Making of the Film'. What does concern us is that Hamish Mahaddie became involved in the embryo project in the latter half of 1966.

True to form, he set about the search for fighter aircraft immediately. Visits to a number of friends in the Ministry of Defence secured the co-operation of that august body – in principle at least. But there was clearly a long way to go. The only fact where the numbers game was concerned was that the RAF only possessed one *Spitfire* and one *Hurricane* capable of flight.

Consequently, the Ministry set up a nationwide survey. Probably to their own surprise they discovered that the RAF still possessed, here and there, quite a large number of *Spitfires* and even some Hurricanes. As a result, Hamish and his helpers managed eventually to identify about one hundred *Spitfires* and eleven *Hurricanes*, in various stages of preservation, but which were at least movable. A few of that number were privately owned.

Many of those veteran aircraft had been allocated to RAF Stations as so-called 'gate guardians', some to suffer the indignity of being run through by plinths, all to undergo the traumatic effects of exposure to the British climate. But from that array of weather-beaten old warriors Hamish discovered that within the bounds of his strictly controlled budget he and the survey team could select a total of a dozen *Spitfires* which were, or could be made, airworthy, plus four *Hurricanes*. More of both types could be brought up to taxying standard or used as background 'props'. Also, a relatively new technique was adopted by moulding glass-fibre full size facsimiles which could be used for static scenes, or as victims of air-raid attacks

It would not be right to divorce from this narrative the extraordinary fact that Hamish Mahaddie's search for authentic military aircraft happily coincided with the decision of the Spanish Government to update its day fighter force. He was told by the British Air Attache in Madrid that the Spanish Air Force was on the point of disposing of a large number of *Buchons* — Licence-built *Me 109s* powered by Rolls Royce *Merlins*. He also learned that the Spaniards also counted in their Order of Battle about two hundred licence-built *Heinkel 111s* which were also equipped with *Merlin* engines. It was just possible that some sort of a deal could be struck which would secure both types for the film.

For the full details of this fascinating turn of fate, reference should again be made to Leonard Moseley's book. It is sufficient to say here that, after flashing to and from Madrid, bearing fortunes in Letters of Credit, making countless international 'phone calls, and attending 'una subasta' — apparently a kind of Dutch auction in Spanish, Hamish achieved his aim. For a while, at least, he presided over the world's largest privately owned air force.

Many of the ground and air sequences were shot using the RAF Stations of West Malling, Bovingdon and Duxford. The completed film was scheduled to contain no less than forty minutes of airborne and associated material, imposing huge demands on a large number of veteran aircraft.

Hamish faced this daunting prospect with no spares backing whatsoever for the British aircraft. They were flown throughout primarily in the hands of professional RAF pilots, many of whom were much more experienced in the fast jet world than high performance pistons. Happily, there was an almost authentic Battle of Britain ambience, a 'press on' spirit which made the best of each day as it came along.

Fortunately, Hamish could rely upon the superlative co-operation of John Simpson, founder of Simpson's Aero Services. Besides being a superb engineer in his own right, Simpson spared no personal effort to keep the aircraft in the air. He drove himself relentlessly throughout that busy summer. He took stock of the unserviceabilities at the end of each day's shooting before tearing off along the motorways with the offending parts to find replacements from here,

Spitfires Reborn

there and everywhere. At times he was forced to snatch a few minutes sleep in rest areas, to arrive back with the dawn to achieve miracles of engineering. Sadly, such self-sacrifice will often take its cruel toll. John Simpson died of a heart attack shortly after the film had been completed.

The situation where engines were concerned was much eased by the presence of Jersey Aviation of St. Helier in the Channel Islands. That company specialises in the supply and maintenance of *Merlin* engines. There must also have been advantage to be gained from the fact that almost all the combined British and Spanish fleets were *Merlin*-powered.

The happy results of that aerial activity were that all sequences were shot as planned, that the picture was completed on time and that, although it had overshot its budget, it made an ultimate profit. The best news was that despite the age of the aircraft, and the scale and type of flying it was necessary to undertake, not one aeroplane was lost.

Once the film was a reality all the actors dispersed to learn their next set of lines. The producers, directors, technicians et al disappeared to wherever they go between pictures. Eventually, all that was left for Hamish to do was to dispose of the aircraft he owned or had hired. The *Heinkel 111s* had their swastikas removed and their Spanish colours replaced, and droned away back to their bases. The *Buchons* and most of the *Spitfires* were put up for sale. One imagines that this was done with a twinge of regret by Hamish, who probably nursed a secret wish to remain a fighter boy for just a little longer. His bank manager, however, had advised otherwise.

So—because a Polish ex-fighter pilot turned film maker wanted to make an historically accurate picture about the greatest aerial battle of all time; because a gutsy little Scot, ex-bomber baron, had the nous to search for and deliver the goods; and because of the goodwill of the RAF, the Spanish Air Force and too many civilians to be listed here, a great film was made.

Perhaps of equal, if not greater, importance, a lot of veteran aircraft were rescued from obscurity and eventual dereliction to live to fly again. Most of them are with us yet, to the enormous pleasure and pride of tens of thousands of aviation enthusiasts.

CHAPTER THREE

Spitfires Down Under

The Royal Air Force has been lucky enough to include many Australians and New Zealanders in its ranks since the day it came into being on 1st April, 1919. Many of them reached the highest ranks. Others gave their lives over the United Kingdom, Europe and elsewhere many thousands of miles from their homes and loved ones. Their help and, in too many cases, sacrifices will never be forgotten by British people in general, and their RAF comrades in particular.

It is not so well known by the layman that there was a time when the RAF became involved in aerial battles over Australian soil. That is probably because reference to a world map might lead one to conclude that for Australia and New Zealand a requirement for single-seater, short range air defence fighters such as the *Spitfire* was almost non-existent. Who and what could possible threaten such distant countries?

That is a reasonable enough observation in the case of New Zealand, where in 1940 even a seaborne threat was hardly a possibility — and it is true to say that today's total *Spitfire* force in that remote and lovely country — one — is more than it has ever had in the past.

Perhaps as far back as 1940 the lack of any obvious threat may have seemed just as realistic an assumption to Australians. That vast, sparsely populated country was, indeed, going to great lengths to

Spitfires Reborn

send its young men away to far-off battle fronts in order to play their part in the war against tyranny.

That assumption of security was to change dramatically with the arrival of the Japanese in what was then the Dutch East Indies (now Indonesia), the nearest point of which was about four hundred miles from Darwin, in the Northern Territories. The fall of Singapore had permitted the invader virtually unfettered access to the archipelago which stretched to the south-east like a road leading to Australia's front door.

It had also denied the Commonwealth forces, such as they now were, all the RAF and RAAF aircraft, and the great majority of trained personnel, previously based in Singapore. Desperate attempts by the United States Navy to ferry *Curtiss P 40s* to the East Indies had further exacerbated the disaster when the seaplane carrier with the relief aircraft on board, the *USS Langley*, was sunk by Japanese aircraft with the loss of thirty-two souls south of Java.

Darwin itself received its first devastating attack on 19th February, 1942. A powerful force of four Japanese aircraft carriers, supported by two battleships, five cruisers and numerous destroyer escorts entered the Timor Sea to deliver the blow. Other enemy air forces flew from the land base of Kendari in the Celebes. Altogether, a total of more than 160 aircraft delivered a body blow against the almost defenceless city. About fifty Australian and US aircraft, mostly caught in transit, were lost; a USN destroyer and eight other ships were sunk.

The threat had suddenly become very real.

It so happened that the attack on defenceless Darwin coincided with a visit to the United Kingdom of Dr H. Evatt, the Australian Minister for External Affairs. He lost no time in calling on the British Prime Minister, the redoubtable Winston Churchill for urgent consultation. The outcome was that the the pressing need for *Spitfires* in Malta and the Middle East would be shelved, at least temporarily, in favour of diverting them to aid Australia. Furthermore, Churchill decreed that Britain's commitment to Australia was to be supreme even if it meant the total sacrifice of operations in the Mediterranean in order to re-deploy the theatre's air and ground forces to Australia in the event of a Japanese invasion.

In May, 1942, Nos. 54, 452 and 457 Squadrons were withdrawn from Fighter Command. Their aircraft, personnel and support equipment, plus three months supplies were embarked in ships of Convoy WS.20 for the long and hazardous journey to the other side of the world.

As the ships ploughed their way slowly southwards events on both sides of the world took on a different shape, causing priorities to be redrawn. Thousands of miles away in the South Pacific the great naval actions at Medway and in the Coral Sea had taken place, markedly reducing the invasion threat to Australia — at least for the time being. Meanwhile, along the African littoral of the Mediterranean, the stronghold of Tobruk had fallen; there was apparently little to stop the German and Italian armies from over-running Egypt, the Suez Canal and the great strategic prize oilfields of the Gulf.

A rapid, even desperate, decision was made as Convoy WS.20 approached the West African coast. Most of its *Spitfires* would be offloaded at Takoradi to be ferried across to the Middle East via Khartoum. The convoy would continue along its planned journey, and the loss of its *Spitfires* would be made up by a special shipment of fifty replacement aircraft. That consignment left the United Kingdom on 5th August to sail westwards through the Panama Canal.

This logistic nightmare was eventually resolved when the personnel of the three squadrons, plus a handful of aircraft which had somehow escaped the Takoradi 'kidnapping', arrived at Melbourne on 13th August. With much hesitation caused by bad weather and inappropriate equipment (the aircraft numbers were made up by issuing *Wirraways* and *Ryan* trainers!), the wing made its way to Darwin. By January 1943 it had been completely re-equipped with its *Spitfire Mk VBs*.

From that time onwards aerial activity around Darwin intensified. Once again, it is history in its own right which should not be dealt with here in any detail. In brief, it can be said that the *Spitfire Mk Vs* gave a good account of themselves in the many daylight combats which took place during the weeks which followed. But the dog-fighting, full throttle climbs and the ever-present dust imposed heavy mechanical strains on the *Merlins,* which in turn gave rise to many unscheduled engine changes and quite a number of airborne failures leading to forced landings.

In the first six months of the air battle over Australia 44 *Spitfires* were lost, but only 17 of those were the result of enemy action. The Japanese, on the other hand, suffered 63 confirmed losses plus 13 probably destroyed.

In October, 1943, the first of the eventual total of 410 *Spitfire Mk VIIIs* began to arrive. By 1944 enemy activity in the Darwin area had virtually ceased and the threat of invasion removed. The air war had moved north-west and decreased in intensity as the allied forces increased in strength and effectiveness throughout South East Asia and the South Pacific.

The writing was already on the wall for the Empire of the Rising Sun.

Although it can be argued that the *Spitfire Vs* and *VIIIs* were not entirely suitable to the ranges and terrain of the area, they managed to hold the line until the danger had receded.

How many of the 650 British-built *Spitfires* which arrived in Australia are still there? As in other countries where the type operated, rumours persist (without any real supporting evidence) that there are 'new' *Spitfires* still in crates bricked up in caves; that some were buried in the sand, or still stand derelict on disused weapons ranges; or that there is treasure to be found by divers around the Great Barrier Reef where many *Mk VIIIs* were consigned.

One would like to think that there may be some truth, somewhere, that hidden caches may one day be uncovered. In the meantime, interest in the *Spitfire* has not died completely. For instance, some of the old comrades of wartime days do their gallant best to keep it alive through the Australian *Spitfire* Association. Sometimes there are odd snippets of news which bring back the memories. Almost certainly bits and pieces of scattered wreckage, scrap metal and souvenir items will emerge as time goes by. Other restored examples may be imported from time to time by wealthy enthusiasts.

In the meantime, let us recount one or two of the interesting stories which, in some way, connect the *Spitfire* with Australia and New Zealand.

STICK-IN-THE-MUD SPITFIRE

22nd December, 1943. The Festive Season. Goodwill to all men seemed like cloud-cuckoo-land to Flying Officer D Grey of the RAF's No 54 Squadron, based at Darwin, Northern Territories, Australia. There was nothing festive about the situation in which he found himself.

Over two and three-quarter hours previously he had taken off from Darwin in *Spitfire Mk V BR545* detailed to patrol the Darwin/Derby area. Since then, he had sweated it out in a cockpit temperature of forty-five degrees C., in conditions of haze which concealed from his vision, the few ground features available for pilot navigation so that he was now—in a word—lost.

To those who have never experienced it, being irrevocably lost in a single-seat fighter, with no help coming from the VHF radio for reasons unknown, is probably one of the most hopeless, harrowing experiences imaginable. The overwhelming feelings of nausea and near-panic grow in inverse proportion to one's fuel remaining. You know that, whatever you do, the single engine will certainly fail within minutes.

Well, for D. Grey, it did. And when that happens in a *Spitfire*, there is only one way to go. To head towards Mother Earth with as much calm and dignity as the situation allows. Open the canopy (given the heat and lack of vision, Grey's would already have been open, anyway), propeller into course pitch, achieve the recommended gliding speed, jettison the slipper tank, trim the aircraft, turn off the now useless magneto switches and fuel tank selectors and look out and aim for the best point of arrival.

'Best', in this case, was a purely relative word. Grey found himself descending quite rapidly over the euphemistically-named Prince Regent River north of Derby. History does not record what the suave Prince Albert's reactions were to having such a rugged, desolate delta being named after him. It is pretty certain that the luckless Grey had a few words to say about it as he scanned the surface for somewhere, anywhere, solid on which to lower his *Spitfire* with some decorum.

He was out of luck. So low now that he was committed to bellying on to what he could now see was acres of grey mud, he locked his straps, held off for as long as he could, and let the doomed aircraft sink to the surface. One imagines that it was not a pretty sight, prop tips spewing wet mud everywhere whilst the *Spitfire* conducted one of those seemingly endless slides so typical of wheel-less forced landings.

But such circumstances do end, and one becomes instantly conscious of the silence falling all around, an unwonted contrast to the constant roar of the *Merlin* until it starved to death a few moments ago. Grey, on the other hand, was very much alive, and considering his position.

It was probably clear to him by now that the area into which he had descended was a mud flat which was so close to the coast that it would undoubtedly be tidal. He would have no way of knowing to what height the water would rise, or how rapidly that transformation would take place. We do know that he made entirely the right decision to inflate his tiny dinghy, secure it to some part of the aircraft, and settle down to await his rescue.

So he waited ... and waited ... and waited. All told, Grey waited for almost four days and nights in that wretched, over-heated humid swamp, cramped in his dinghy, going up and down with the tides. One does not know if he ever realised that crocodiles had made the area their home, or if there were any members of the human race near enough to help. Some say that he was eventually spotted by aboriginees — probably pearl fishers. We do know that he was picked up by a *Walrus* amphibian on Christmas Day.

It is to be hoped that as he revelled in his bath, clean clothes, and first meal for four days, he was not troubled by any pangs of conscience with regard to his *Spitfire Mk V BR545*, lying for ever mud-bound in the Prince Regent River.

Forever? Well, maybe not quite. Forty-five years later, Wing Commander Jim de Bomford, of the Royal Australian Air Force, led a party of twelve RAAF servicemen and one RAN officer on a carefully prepared expedition to salvage whatever was left of the *Spitfire*. They set sail from Broome in the salvage vessel *Wandi Two* on their two-and-a-half day trip to the Regent River.

They were prepared for most contingencies, including anti-crocodile measures. They had been briefed not to kill any creature whilst carrying out their salvage work — but they had equipped themselves with a variety of firearms which would at least scare most wildlife and, they fervently hoped, deter the giant reptiles. They were sensitive to the fact that a tourist from the United States, one Ginger Meadows, had fallen victim to a gigantic crocodile just a few months previously.

The barge duly arrived on station, despite some reluctance from the engines whilst in passage. The *Spitfire* was below the water, but well marked with a white football-sized buoy. As the tide went out, *BR545* slowly became visible.

On the second day, as soon as tidal conditions allowed, armed lookouts were posted around the deck for more than five hours while a working party laboured in the heat and slime trying to clear the clinging mud from the wreck. The intention was to attach flotation bags to the old aircraft in order to lift it with the aid of the incoming tide.

Alas, that excellent idea came to nought. Once the water started to put pressure on the bags, they sprung leaks one by one as they were pierced by spiky oyster shells which had adhered to the aircraft's structure. A whole day's work had gained them virtually nothing.

On the third day, following the failure of the flotation bags, the salvage party decided to sever the heavy *Merlin* engine with its propeller still attached, from the fuselage. That was done with some difficulty, and the heavy engine was attached to two powerful winches which inched it towards the vessel. During this part of the operation the rescuers discovered the pilot's oxygen mask, a compass and two almost unblemished *Dunlop* tyres. To their surprise, during the amputation of the engine from the rest of the aircraft, they also found that the hydraulic lines still contained oil under pressure.

The engine is successfully brought on deck

Spitfires Reborn

The process was tortuous and physically exhausting. The heat was excruciating, their body sweat attracted every type of flying, biting insect imaginable, and progress was slow enough to keep the team on the job continuously for more than twenty-four hours. The engine was brought to the sill of the ramp just in time to prevent it from again being swallowed by the tide; it was not until dawn on the fourth day that exhausted workers were able to make it secure.

Time was not in their favour. Their provisions were running low, and fresh water could become a difficulty, even though it was strictly rationed for drinking purposes only. The team's leader decided that another attempt should be made with the flotation bags now that the engine had been removed. It took a further six hours to attach them, always with an eye on the incoming tide. Success came as the water started to ooze beneath the fuselage.

The rescuers watched, hardly daring to breathe. As the water level rose, the buoyancy of the bags, plus that of the salvage vessel itself, stirred the old *Spitfire*. She seemed to stretch herself like an old lady who has remained in the same chair for too long. The water surrounded her as she rose slowly from the cloying mud which had been her captor for so many years. The excitement and glee of the salvage crew can be imagined.

Slowly the winches revolved, edging the fuselage and wings towards the barge's ramp. Then, with total success in their grasp, a flotation bag burst, allowing a large percentage of the aircraft to fall back into the water. The tide was already turning by this time, so there was nothing to do but to allow the *Spitfire* to settle back onto the mud once more.

It was now essential to abandon the site within the next few hours as they were by that time without any provisions. Wing Commander de Bomford decided that the only way ahead lay in deep surgery. They would amputate the starboard wing.

The operation commenced. The expedition's cook—with nothing to cook—was in a dinghy helping Flying Officer Mike Roberts to secure a rope when they became chillingly aware of large, black shapes moving slowly through the murky water very close to their slender craft. Roberts yelled to the armed lookout, scrambling to his feet and pointing frenziedly at the nearest man-eater about ten feet away.

The small boat lurched and Roberts disappeared from view. It looked for all the world as if he was sharing the river with the man-eater crocodiles. The crew aboard the salvage vessel pulled for all they were worth on the dinghy's mooring rope, while all available gunners blasted off in a deafening fusillade. During the turmoil, Fg. Off. Roberts lay where he had fallen, in the bottom of the boat until, much to the relief of everyone, he felt it safe to re-emerge.

The party was now determined to finish the job they had come to do. While the crocodiles slithered about the mangrove swamp, or occasionally carried out a reconnaissance, the men laboured away throughout the night. By the time dawn signalled the coming of another long, hot day only the cockpit and the port wing remained to be brought aboard.

Three of the team work to bring the severed cockpit on board.

Encouraged by their success, and with visions of their imminent departure for home foremost in their minds, the party wasted no time in securing the remaining portions of salvage. At last, with everything secure, they weighed anchor with a sigh of relief, waved farewell to the reptiles with whom they'd shared the swamp for four days, and set sail for Broome, a shower and a good meal.

After forty-five years, *Spitfire Mk V BR545* had at last returned to dry land. She may never fly again — perhaps that would be expect-

Spitfires Reborn

ing too much—but she and her story will be greeted with wonderment over the years to come.

The only poignant reflection is that it is a matter of great regret that her pilot, Flight Lieutenant D. Grey, was never able to re-acquaint himself with that willing mount he had been forced to deposit on the mud. He survived the war, but died at a sadly young age during the '60s.

Another 'down under' Spitfire—Mk XVI—TB863—at home in New Zealand. She is seen here during her post-restoration air test in the hands of Stephen Grey. The aircraft is now owned by Tim Wallis of Wanuka (for more details, see 'Spitfires and Saviours' chapter).

CHAPTER FOUR

The Two Graces

E. N. Grace—Nick, as he was universally known—was born in Cheshire on 6th August, 1936. His father, a wine merchant, was a highly principled man who took pains to instil the virtues of honesty, learning and self-sufficiency into his four children, two girls and two boys. Of the latter, Christopher was the eldest by eleven months.

Christopher and Nick, who were close in friendship as well as years, attended Prior Park College, Bath, for their senior schooling after which Nick decided to develop his interests in engineering. He took a place at Loughborough so to do. Shortly after completing his degree in the subject he became eligible for two years compulsory National Service.

During that period in army uniform, Nick Grace served in the Parachute Regiment, taking an active part in the Anglo-French Suez intervention which resulted from the nationalisation of the Canal by Colonel Nasser, the then President of Egypt.

Also, during his two years with the Colours, Nick had become actively involved in the sport of motor-cycle scrambling. The experience enabled him to lead a very successful scrambling career with the BSA works team after his demobilisation. He also took an interest in a garage which specialised in maintaining Rolls Royce cars. The venture became successful largely as a result of Nick's management and engineering skills.

Spitfires Reborn

It was during this time that Nick bought a *Ginetta G4* racing car. He was the genius who placed it on the racing map, utilising his design engineering skills with both the car body and the engine. He won many formula races at Brands Hatch, Debden and Goodwood.

Despite his success, it seems that Nick Grace felt a need to widen his horizons, for he decided to emigrate to Australia under the 'ten pounds' scheme which was operating at that time for citizens of the United Kingdom. Once there, he designed and built the *Brolga*, another successful racing and sports car. He raced it himself with the result that his brain-child became widely known and much sought after. Naturally, as it was hand-crafted, only a few models were produced; those remaining are now collectors' pieces.

Having achieved his engineering objectives where the *Brolga* car was concerned, he turned his attention to boat-building. He had always enjoyed sailing, and Australia is the ideal place for it. Consequently, Nick set up a business near Sydney. It was not long before he was turning out his own designs of a sailing dinghy and a catamaran at the rate of one each day.

Nick Grace had long harboured an ambition to fly. In 1952, he qualified as a glider pilot and later gained his full Private Pilot's Licence. Having done so he was able to add crop-spraying and delivery flying to his list of activities. Indeed, it was during one of those missions that he first met Carolyn.

Carolyn Mansfield (as she was then) was living on her family's 5,000 acre shorthorn stud farm at Goulbarn, New South Wales. At the age of eighteen, the aircraft that the family used for shopping expeditions in Sydney held limited interest for her. When Nick arrived in a *Tiger Moth* on the crop-dusting strip her beloved horse on which she was riding when she met him took second place. The aircraft and Nick had kindled her desire to fly vintage aircraft.

Nick decided that the time had come to return to his homeland, and that he did, with Carolyn. Once again he became involved in the boat-building business in that most delightful of havens, Guernsey in the British Channel Islands, building 48-foot and 30-foot sailing yachts to a design by Van de Stadt, a top man in the yachting world. Once again, Nick's engineering skills were able to come to the fore.

The Two Graces

Starting with only the drawings, Nick and Carolyn, on their own initially, built the first plug, then mould and, finally, the complete 48-foot yacht. It was the first of many very successful cruising and racing yachts.

Something had long existed in Nick's mind as a remote wish, to one day fly a *Spitfire*. Like many other youngsters whose childhood was conditioned by the shadow of war, he was fascinated by the sky and aviation in general. In particular, the *Spitfire* had excited both his aesthetic and engineering instincts. Now, so many years after the conflict, those appetites remained; his deep desire to fly a *Spitfire* was undiminished. But no longer was it a matter of picking one up for scrap metal prices. The interest in historic aircraft had increased in inverse proportion to the diminishing supply. In any case, Nick could not fully satisfy his ambition to own and pilot a *Spitfire* by simply putting cash on the table in a second-hand market. That would not have fulfilled his desire for an engineering challenge.

In the fullness of time the opportunity arose. A *Spitfire* with a long and chequered came up for disposal in 1979. Originally built at Castle Bromwich as a *Spitfire LF Mk IX, ML407* joined the RAF on 23rd April, 1944. She flew operationally with various units of the New Zealand, Free French, Polish, Belgian and Norwegian air forces. She carried out 176 operational sorties, and was accredited with shooting down the first enemy aircraft over the D-Day landings

Her fighting days over, *ML407* was stored in the United Kingdom until 1950. She was then sold back to her makers, Vickers Armstrongs (Supermarine) who converted her to a two-seat trainer as part of a contract for the Irish Air Corps. In 1960, she was retired from active flying for the second time, and relegated for use as a 'training airframe' at the apprentices' school. After a further hiatus, *ML407* was offered for sale in 1968.

A buyer was found, and the old fighter was shipped to the UK and put in store at Cricklewood, London, until 1970. She was again sold, moved to Flimwell, Shoreham and, eventually, to join the Strathallan Collection in Scotland. There she languished in store for a further nine years.

Nick and Carolyn travelled north to Scotland to take a look at the pieces. There they found a fuselage, a set of mainplanes, with

Spitfires Reborn

countless other components crated but which, in toto, purported to constitute a complete *Spitfire*. The whole shipment was loaded into a couple of Pickford's vans and moved south to St Merryn in Cornwall.

There followed five years of the most extreme test of dedication that one could possibly imagine. The airframe components, lying unprotected in various stores for the previous eleven years had, at some stage, been stripped of paint and covered in a coat of primer. All the components needed to be inspected and properly logged — thousands of bits and pieces to be recognised and listed.

Nick decided that, in order to restore *ML407* to safe flying condition of the standards that he demanded as engineer and pilot, he would dismantle and inspect every last square inch of the aircraft's structure.

Of course, throughout the whole operation, he had to retain his business as his only means of earning a livelihood. That meant working on the aircraft whenever he was able. During the five years, he somehow managed to devote some 10,000 man hours to the gigantic task he had set himself.

Although there was a fund of engineering know-how in his make-up, particularly in car building, Nick had never before been involved in such depth with aircraft. Now, here he was, surveying thousands of bits and pieces strewn across the hangar floor, hoping it would all amount to a complete aircraft in the end. The only way to find out was to start.

Carolyn remembers viewing the scene and asking, "Where are you going to begin?" Nick shook his head in some puzzlement and simply said, "I don't know. I'll just start."

It is not the aim here to go into great technical detail concerning this immense task. It is, perhaps, a suitably graphic illustration of the enormity of the operation to report that all the original magnesium rivets which had suffered internal corrosion, had to be drilled out and replaced. All other areas of corrosion had to be identified, and treated or replaced by new metal. All electrical wiring — miles of it — had to be renewed; every inch of the plumbing — hydraulic, fuel, pneumatic, and oil systems — had to be inspected and replaced as necessary.

The Two Graces

Piece by piece the work progressed. The news of Nick's progress filtered through to others with similar interests. Some even made the journey to distant Cornwall to see for themselves. The patience of both Nick and Carolyn is still to be marvelled at in retrospect.

At last the thrilling moment came when the workshop doors were pushed back; with engine cowlings removed the Grace family rolled out their pride and joy into the sunlight and bracing air of North Cornwall in readiness for the first engine run after restoration.

Nick climbed into the front cockpit. This culminating moment — this watershed — after five years of unbelievably hard and exacting engineering, with all its highs and lows, was intensely exciting. If all went well, all those hours would be totally rewarded: if not — well, it would be back to the drawing board.

Nick's hands moved carefully but positively around the cockpit and instrument panel. Mixture to rich, throttle 'cracked', fuel main tanks on, contents sufficient, pneumatic supply OK, brakes on and locked, stick hard back. A look to the front and rear to see that all was clear. A few smooth strokes on the *Kigas* (primer) pump to whet the *Merlin's* appetite, and all was ready.

"Switches on. Contact!"

The traditional warning cry told all within earshot that the engine was live. With his left hand on the throttle, his right hand moved the guard covers away from the booster and starter buttons. Nick pressed them both firmly and simultaneously. The four propeller blades turned. The low-pitched murmur of well-oiled bearings accompanied the rotation. Then came the slight hesitation of the blades as the small puffs of white smoke were expelled through the exhaust ports.

The engine fired, coughed, fired again — and burst into full life. Exhaust smoke, with the characteristic, slightly acrid smell that only a highly-tuned powerful piston can provide, whirled away and was torn to shreds by the slipstream. The great engine settled into its smooth song of life.

Quite soon, after more than twenty years of near neglect on the ground until resuscitated by her proud owner, *Spitfire Mk T9 ML407* would once again lift herself free of Mother Earth to regain her rightful place in the air.

With the likelihood of *ML407* coming up for her post-rebuild test flight just over the horizon Nick decided that he should 'consider his position', as the expression has it.

By 1985 he had accrued a considerable number of flying hours in light or 'domestic' types of aircraft; his most recent experience since the move to Guernsey had been mainly concerned with his own *de Havilland Dove* which he used for commuting to and from England. Nick realised that there would be an enormous gulf between such aircraft with which he was familiar, and a high performance piston fighter, and that it would be a good idea if he could arrange to get a little time with the latter if possible.

That presented something of a problem as his own *Spitfire* was, in fact, the only flyable two-seater in the country. There was, however, a two-seater *Hawker Sea Fury* owned by the Royal Navy, and Nick rightly thought that some experience in that impressive aircraft, properly supervised, would stand him in good stead. Consequently, he made his approach, explained the position, and received the promise of maximum co-operation. It was thought that five hours would be sufficient to do the job.

On the appointed day Nick checked in with the RN Historic Flight at the Royal Naval Air Station at Yeovilton, Wiltshire. After briefing he went with his flight-check pilot to the *Fury* for the first of his allotted one-hour sorties. Under normal circumstances, that would consist of nothing more than simple familiarisation. After getting airborne they left the circuit to carry out a few steep turns, and a demonstration of the aircraft's systems generally. They then returned so that Nick could get to know the various power settings and speeds for circuit work. (That is, of course, fundamental to the successful flying of any aircraft—particularly a powerful piston). It is apparent that Nick, as one could expect, was an outstanding student. On completion of the flight, which included several 'touch-and-go' landings and the odd overshoot, the instructor told Nick that in his opinion that one hour was all that was needed.

Armed with the experience of his *Sea Fury* trip, Nick returned to St Merryn to put the final touches to *ML407*. In fact, by this time he had painted the *Spitfire* using No 485 Squadron code *OU-V.* The letter was the initial of Vicki, the wife of Johnnie Houlton, one of the aircraft's original pilots of World War 2 days. Thus, *ML407* again came to be known as Vicki.

On 16th April, 1985, a quarter of a century after her last flight, the carefully rebuilt *Spitfire* was rolled out, Nick started and checked the *Merlin* with great care and, one can be sure, considerable excitement. Then, for the first time, with the healthy bellow of her engine singing in his ears, Nick took his aircraft into the air.

The flight was an unqualified success. The Graces again saw the moment as a watershed, but this time it was one to involve the complete family. With her newly certificated status and civilian registration, *G-LFIX*, the time had come to move the base of operations further east.

The remainder of 1985 passed in a bustle of activity and changing circumstances. There will be many American readers who will remember their wartime airfield of Westhampnett, a wartime satellite of historic Tangmere. Now known as Goodwood, it was to become a convenient home for *ML407*, situated as it is within reasonable flying time to most other airfields which host the major flying displays.

That was an important point. The Graces had done their homework regarding costs, and were fully aware that it is one thing to buy and restore a *Spitfire*, using one's own time and labour (although even that is expensive enough), but quite another to maintain and operate it thereafter. Landing fees, handling charges, fuel costs and, above all, insurance coverage add up to something in the region of twenty-eight thousand pounds each year. Statutory checks, also, have to be taken into account. After some five hundred hours flying time the Rolls Royce *Merlin* has to undergo a major overhaul. That sees little change from forty-five thousand pounds at today's reckoning. Another very sensitive and potentially costly area is the propeller, which is always prone to damage from stones, unwary birds, or even 'pecking'.

As times have changed the shapes of aeroplanes so radically over the years, it is perhaps as well to take a little time here to explain this latter point.

The *Spitfire*, in company with almost all its contemporaries, is a so-called 'tail dragger' (to use a modern and inelegant expression). That means that on the ground it rests on two main wheels, complete

Spitfires Reborn

with brakes, situated beneath the wing's leading edges, and a small and freely castering tail-wheel. That configuration causes at least two major disadvantages, particularly in the case of an aircraft powered by a lengthy in-line engine such as the *Merlin* or *Griffon*. Forward visibility on the ground is seriously impaired, and the aircraft's centre of gravity can be quite close to the main undercarriage structure. When manoeuvring on the ground (taxying, landing or taking-off), great care must be taken to avoid any heavy braking, intentional or by some other means such as running into soft ground or even long grass. The combined effect of the aircraft's momentum, the weight of the engine and propeller's reduction gear, and the closeness of the main wheels and the centre of gravity can cause the aircraft to pivot forward and the propeller blades to strike the ground, likened by some to a hen foraging for food. Hence the expression 'pecking'.

Given the condition of some of the wartime fields and sandy strips from which *Spitfires* were required to operate, (and, perhaps, the inexperience of the pilots), pecking was a lamentably frequent occurrence. The sight of the slim, normally graceful shape of a *Spitfire* tilted on to its broken propeller and main wheels, with its pilot, both furious and embarrassed as he surveyed the damage, would be the cue for all his fellows to chant ungraciously and raucously: "There he goes, on his nose! Got his brakes on I suppose."

To return to our theme. Wooden propellers striking the ground whilst rotating under engine power almost invariably mean the replacement of all its blades. At today's prices that can mean up to fifty-five thousand pounds. There is, incidentally, a certain irony in the fact that today's source of new *Spitfire* propeller blades is the German firm of Hofmann!

Even a seemingly simple occurrence, such as a punctured or cut main wheel tyre can induce a little despondency. Simple it may be, (and one hundred and forty pounds a time may not sound a lot if one says it quickly), but as an owner is never likely to get many more than thirty landings out of a tyre, changes are all too frequent. That is despite the fact that the wheels are freely rotational in the sense that they do not have to suffer imposed mechanical accelerations as applied to cars. They do, nevertheless, need to withstand an instant rotation on landing from zero to that required to sustain about four tons of aircraft at a forward speed of, say, 60 m.p.h..

The Two Graces

So, it's an expensive business. Nick Grace quite understandably and rightly was determined that the object of his handiwork, the lovely Vicki would have to contribute towards her upkeep. She would have to show off her beauty at major airshows, in advertisements, and in films. She would have to try to attract donations of money, equipment and services. She would, if at all possible, need substantial sponsorship.

Gradually everything came together. Happily, a mutual acceptable arrangement was arrived at with Leslie and Godwin, a well-known company of aeronautical and general insurance brokers whose logo is proudly displayed by Vicki. Television South, drawn by the intriguing reincarnation of the beautiful and historic aircraft which had taken up residence in their area, made an excellent feature documentary aptly entitled "The Perfect Lady".

The eventful year, for the Graces, of 1985, came to an end. Vicki was ready and waiting, poised for an equally exciting new year. 1986 was to see the 50th anniversary of the first flight of the *Spitfire* prototype from Eastleigh—and she, Nick and Carolyn intended to join in the celebrations.

5th March, 1986. A reluctant dawn slowly transformed the inky blackness of night into a dank, gloomy day. A petulant, gusty breeze hustled ragged, low clouds before it, trailing murky curtains of drizzle over the Solent and the city of Southampton.

It was a discouraging start to a day when many plans were to come together in celebration of that day, fifty years previously, when the diminutive Supermarine Type 300, *K5054*, the prototype *Spitfire*, skipped her way across the turf at Eastleigh in the hands of Captain 'Mutt' Summers, to rise dartlike into the air for the first time ever.

The recently formed *Spitfire* Society, appropriately based in Southampton, had reached the conclusion that the anniversary had to be commemorated come what may. A similar occasion concerning the *Hawker Hurricane* had come and gone the previous year with hardly anyone noticing, and that was not to be repeated.

Fortunately, the Society received the whole-hearted co-operation of the Eastleigh Borough Council, the Eastleigh Airport authorities, and the Southampton City Council. Invitations had gone out to all *Spitfire* owners to attend a Fly-in on the day, and a small static exhibition had been arranged. TVS and BBC television and radio commentators had sited their cameras and microphones. By 8 a.m. a senior representative of the *Spitfire* Society had laid a wreath on the steps of the simple memorial standing on the site of the old bombed-out Supermarine factory beneath the concrete mass of the Itchen road bridge.

As it always will, the word had spread during the days running up to the anniversary. A great deal of interest was aroused, and much unsought publicity had emerged. In consequence, what had been intended as a private celebration had already snowballed into an enormous concourse homing in to Eastleigh from all points of the compass. To the organisers of the event it was the first and extremely graphic illustration of the universal pulling power of the *Spitfire*.

March is not the ideal time of the year to arrange a flying event — particularly one involving veteran aircraft. Consequently, only a maximum of five *Spitfires* were expected, with a non-flyer on exhibition in the shelter of a hangar. That would, nevertheless, represent the largest number of the type to gather together since the early '50s. Included in the five was Nick Grace's Vicki.

The rain fell steadily on to the already sodden airfield. The clouds hung like a pall a mere three hundred feet above the forest of golf umbrellas sheltering the expectant mass. Fortunately, one *Spitfire* had arrived the day previously, the rare and immaculate *PR Mk XI PL983*, then owned by a one-time Free French pilot, the late Roland Fraissinet, later to tragically lose his life in an attempt to rescue by helicopter an injured English skier in the Massif. The pristine aircraft, glinting in the rain, was enough to awaken the nostalgia in the bosoms of all those present.

The Battle of Britain Memorial Flight had tried but, with their strict rules about the avoidance of precipitation, Wg. Cdr. John Ward of the Battle of Britain Memorial Flight had diverted to Benson to await better tidings. Tony Bianchi, with the *Spitfire Mk I AR213*, had just as prudently left it sheltering in the hangar at Booker. Nick Grace had made a noble effort but had decided, in the end, to sit out the weather at Micheldever, which itself was pretty sodden.

But bad things, as well as good, eventually come to an end. The cold front decided to take itself off towards the east, the cloud base went up, and the persistent rain reduced to an occasional fine drizzle.

The Two Graces

Suddenly, an air of excitement ran around the assembled company. Umbrellas were stowed, fingers pointed towards the north, and over the field swept John Ward in the *Spitfire Mk II, P7350*, accompanied by that almost indescribable whoosh of a perfectly tuned *Merlin*. Things were happening.

Not far away to the north Nick, aware of the partial clearance, was making ready for the few minutes flight to Eastleigh. Carefully avoiding the worst of the water lying on the surface of the field at Micheldever, he turned into wind and very carefully eased the throttle forward and, with the stick well back, splashed his way into the air.

With scarcely time to close the canopy, he followed the line of the main road south to Eastleigh, was given clearance to land, and joined the downwind leg to carry out pre-landing checks.

Airspeed, 140 knots. Canopy, open and secure. Undercarriage down. Pitch, fully forward. Supercharger, red light out. Carburettor air intake closed. Fuel, main cock on, contents checked, booster on. Then, turning on to the final approach, flaps down and retrim as required. Brake pressure checked.

Looking ahead, with the last of the drizzle crazing the windscreen, Nick had the glistening runway with its centre white dashes well positioned. Coming over the railway marshalling yards, the engine making its characteristic popping as the power setting was reduced, Nick, in the smooth air following the rain, knew that this was going to be a good one. Over the threshold, at exactly the right height, he eased the stick back, bringing the throttle back to the stop as he did so. To his intense satisfaction he felt all three wheels touch the runway simultaneously. A perfect three-pointer

And then the world fell in. The nose, instead of blocking his view, started to lower. With the stick hard back, Nick's hand flicked the ignition switches to the 'off' position without really having yet assessed what was happening. The nose continued to drop until, with the airscrew still turning of its own momentum, the first small splinters of laminated wood flew into the air. As he turned the fuel cock off, the pilot heard the tortured scrape of immaculately painted metal as the belly of his beautiful Vicki met the unyielding surface of the runway.

There was nothing more to do but wait for the ignominious slide to come to an end in its own good time. It did, and the silence was only broken by the sound of the approaching crash vehicles.

Nick climbed out, walked away, and turned to look at his aeroplane. Without doubt he experienced similar feelings to those felt by others who had suffered similar misfortunes—if only one could live the last minute over again!

But one cannot—and one finds some quick consolation in the realisation that one's vulnerable piece of hardware is, after all, still in one piece, and will live to fly another day.

'Vicki' after the accident at Southampton's Eastleigh Airport.

Nick Grace was not a man to allow misfortune, or even temporary aberration, to hold him up for too long. Vicky on her belly was a prospect which he found quite abhorrent. It was unnatural, undignified, and not at all compatible with the person who had so recently brought her back to life. Furthermore, he had no idea why she should have fallen down on the job.

But the show had to go on—and at that moment Vicki, lying slightly to the right of the runway centre-line was tending to obstruct the smooth operation of a busy provincial airport. Fortunately, although these days such incidents are happily rare, the drill is well-practised by all good airfield crash/rescue crews.

Having ascertained that the *Spitfire* was not about to go up in flames, and that, despite the indignity of her pose, damage appeared to be minimal, her front end was lifted from the ground allowing the main landing gear to be extended and locked into position. It was then a quick and simple matter to tow and manhandle her out of harm's way.

Naturally, Nick puzzled over the incident for some time. His first assessment was that somewhere in the system a mechanical failure had occurred, such as a fracture. That would have presented a serious problem at the very commencement of a new and important season as it would clearly prevent any other flying until full corrective action had been taken. Exhaustive tests, however, failed to disclose anything untoward in the aircraft's systems.

In the meantime, Nick racked his brains for an alternative answer to the mystery. Eventually he said to Carolyn: "I've looked at it from every angle — and nobody knows what makes Vicki tick better than I do. I'm pretty sure now that, immediately before touch-down during the pre-landing checks I must have accidentally selected the gear up instead of switching the main fuel tank on."

That would seem to be the most likely answer, distasteful though it was. As it happens, in *ML407* the conventional *Spitfire* undercarriage selector box is in the rear cockpit. Nick, of course, was flying from the front cockpit where the selector consists of a simple two-way 'up or down' control which is situated immediately adjacent to the main fuel tank selector.

It is typical of Nick Grace to be quite ready to admit to himself and anyone else interested that he could have easily fallen foul of that old bogey, pilot error. If it had not occurred to him before, it did then that a pilot's mis-management of his aircraft can, in itself, be nothing more than pressing the wrong button, or selecting the wrong switch, but the probable effect in the exacting business of flying can be instant and disastrous. There are very few other occupations so totally unforgiving of error. All of us who have flown anything at all, but particularly in high performance aircraft of any sort, have erred from time to time. When we have been lucky we have learned a lesson with no harm done, but usually second chances are not available.

Spitfires Reborn

Nick had told himself on final approach that '...this will be a good one'. So it would have been under normal circumstances. So good, in fact, that Vicki had lost a mere few inches of each laminated wood propeller blades, a scrape of paint from the underside of the radiators and oil cooler, a dented wing fairing, and that was about all.

To most pilots, an aircraft grounded because of unserviceability is anathema. Characteristically, Nick set about correcting the situation immediately. Within the week he had visited Germany personally to arrange for the replacement of the propeller blades. He also received customary and generous co-operation from Rotol Dowty in this country who assisted and advised him on refitting the airscrew. At the same time, the slight damage to the airframe was quickly repaired.

The consequence of all these activities was that Vicki was 'back on the line' in a matter of days, none the worse.

The unfortunate mishap now behind them, life for the Graces and their charge settled down to a busy, enjoyable yet demanding round of appearances at the many airshows and similar functions which fill the summer season in Europe. In the aftermath of six years of global war, and living in the ever-present shadow of nuclear deterrence there was, and is, a widespread interest in yesterday's military aircraft which fought the battles of World War 2, and today's expensive, modern equipment which recent history has again demonstrated are still vital to prevent further disasters.

With Vicki fully fit and performing well, Nick's interest in a wider field of old aircraft increased. He turned his attention to a close relative of the *Spitfire's* erstwhile protagonist, the Spanish-built *Buchon*, virtually an *Me109* powered by a Rolls Royce *Merlin* engine. In their short relationship he was not overly impressed. Despite the aircraft's creditable performance it could be difficult to handle and did not, he thought, possess the *Spitfire's* aesthetic grace and pilot compatibility.

Vicki spent much of her time at Goodwood, set amidst the lush grassland and wooded hills of Sussex. She was now the only surviving *Spitfire* in that area from which hundreds had operated in the cause of freedom. Naturally, she excited great interest and admiration whenever she was rolled out of the hangar.

To the proud owner life had settled into an enjoyable and successful rhythm. The greatest challenge he had ever faced—the acquisition and flying of a *Spitfire*— had been met and overcome. It had taken years of effort in cold, drafty hangars, but the reward was there in all her pristine elegance.

Nick knew her well. Every square inch of her smooth skin, every murmur of her engine, every single rivet which had gone to make up her lovely shape, was there because he had willed it.

'Vicki' the Spitfire T.9 ML407 two-seater, at Boscombe Down, 1990 (Bayliss)

One evening in 1988 after his usual busy day, Nick headed for home and a few hours relaxation. As he drove along the leafy by-roads of Sussex he must have been deeply content with the twists and turns his life had taken thus far. Apart from the few sadnesses and disappointments which are occasionally inevitable, he had experienced a life of challenge, adventure and success. He had travelled the world, soldiered in foreign parts, sailed boats of his own design, built motor cars, rebuilt a classic fighter plane, and had shared a happy family life.

Spitfires Reborn

Tragically, that short, routine journey was never completed. Nick Grace, engineer and pilot, lost his life instantly in a collision with an oncoming car when its driver lost control.

But Carolyn and the children remained.

Whatever tragedies have to be endured it is one of life's ironies — or, perhaps, savings — that it will doggedly carry on. Ignoring the brutal fact that one of the lynch-pins of one's life has disappeared, one who had seemed quite indestructible, day will follow night, the telephone still rings, the postman calls, bills have to be paid, children must be fed and clothed, weeks grow into months. Although the hurt, the anger at the unfairness of it all, will never go away, in the end it has to be contained.

The time came when Carolyn Grace had to think positively about the future. She had her Cashmere Goat farm in Sussex well established and recognised as a leading stud in Cashmere breeding, although still fighting for permission for the house that she and Nick had planned, the children were settled at school. It was now necessary to make one or two fundamental decisions concerning the aircraft.

It was clear that she was, amongst other things, deprived of the engineering and training skills which were Nick's, but Vicki was already in good shape and, with luck, would require only straightforward maintenance to keep her flying for some time to come. There are a number of highly-skilled companies in England quite capable of organising and carrying out a planned maintenance scheme for veteran aircraft. Indeed, one such, Historic Flying Ltd., was a near neighbour at Audley End Airfield, near Saffron Walden, Essex. Duxford, the one-time 12 Group Station of Battle of Britain fame, and now home to the Imperial War Museum, also houses many historic aircraft, and the skilled people who look after them.

So Carolyn Grace arrived at an important decision. She already had the services of a pilot of suitable experience who would be available to fly and exhibit the aircraft. She would also do what she knew Nick very much wanted her to do, complete her training which would enable her to fly Vicki herself.

This last, brave decision must have given Carolyn much food for thought. Although by that time she had come a long way since those

The Two Graces

early days in Australia when she and Nick had first met, the level of her flying experience was still at a fairly basic level, and she had learned from Nick that there is a wealth of difference between the sort of flying she had achieved, and that which she was about to attempt. Nick had taught her to fly and had, over three years, whenever the opportunity arose, given her whatever limited time was possible in the *Spitfire*.

Fortunately, Peter Kinsey who, when he was not flying *Boeing 737s* for Britannia Airways, loved nothing more than to get his hands on a *Spitfire*. Carolyn told him of her wish, not only to keep Vicki flying as a living memorial to her late husband, but to do her very best to do some of it herself.

Peter Kinsey went along with her ideas, and it was not long before he began to pass on to Carolyn as much of his own expertise with *Spitfires* as he could. Carolyn was a ready pupil, and grew in confidence and experience the more she flew with Peter. The day arrived when Peter thought to himself: 'She's got it. The aircraft's behaving itself. The weather's good.'

No-one who has ever flown a *Spitfire* will forget that first solo ride. Carolyn, unlike RAF aircrew, had been given the considerable advantage of dual instruction in a two-seater *Spitfire*. She was, nevertheless, in a somewhat similar position to wartime trainees, at least in 1940 and 1941, most of whom had little more than seventy or eighty hours solo in elementary and basic types before launching themselves into the air in their first single-seater *Spitfire*.

A Television South film crew was standing by to record her first *Spitfire* solo flight. It had been Nick's wish that the event should be well-known. (The result, a film called 'Going Solo' was presented in the Series 'The Human Factor'.)

Now, her moment had come. For the first time ever, she sat alone in that familiar cockpit. As, under her command, Vicki bumped and swayed across the turf towards the runway threshold it may be that Carolyn heard, above the healthy note of the *Merlin*, the calm, encouraging voice of Nick urging her forward.

She lined Vicki up for take-off. A last minute check around the cockpit to ensure that all was as it should be. A final look all around the aircraft and the air above. Then, with the customary minimum of forward vision she moved the throttle forward, heard again that throaty surge of power from the *Merlin*, and, as Vicki accelerated forward, kept her nose along the line of the runway by the use of rudder. With the stick in the neutral position it was not long before the tail rose, giving her a better view forward. Then she was smoothing out the last few attempts by Vicki to bounce her into the air until the rumble from the wheels ceased, everything went smooth, and they were airborne.

As the airspeed moved rapidly towards the climbing speed of 155 knots (180 m.p.h.) Carolyn spared a hand to raise the undercarriage, and then make whatever elevator and rudder trim changes were necessary.

A little later, back on the downwind leg prior to landing and, knowing in the back of her mind that this would be an even more demanding test of her abilities than the take-off, she took extra care to check the aircraft's height and its position and track relative to the runway. OK so far.

Now, the checks before landing, quickly but correctly as the *Spitfire* gobbled up the distance to the ideal turn-in point. Airspeed, power, trim. Final checks before touch-down. The runway seemed to approach at the speed of light. Now, flare out and check. Don't let her balloon upwards. Hold steady. Stick coming back—and back—and back as the nose comes up, preventing any forward vision again. Carolyn was just making that last, fervent hope that she'd got it right, and that she wasn't, in fact, still thirty feet off the surface, when the three wheels rumbled as the aircraft touched down. With a great sense of achievement welling up inside her, she corrected any tendency for Vicki to swing by coarse use of rudder until she gently brought the aircraft to a halt.

She had done it. She had set herself perhaps the greatest challenge possible, and she had won! Carolyn Grace knew that Nick would have approved, that he would have been as proud of her feat as she was herself.

There will, of course, be other challenges in the years that lie ahead. Things may not always go smoothly. But Carolyn Grace, *Spitfire* pilot, knows, as we know, that she has the spirit to tackle any problems, and conquer them.

CHAPTER FIVE

The Micheldever Story

Tucked away amidst the fields and woodlands of rural Hampshire is what we like to think of as a typical English village. It goes under the rather quaint name of Micheldever which meant, 1,600 years ago in its original Anglo-Saxon, 'bog-stream'. Today it has a population of around 1,500 people, many of whom are city commuters, for it lies within one hour's travelling time from Central London. It is bordered on all sides by busy arteries of road and rail, and overhead by busy air routes.

Micheldever is, nevertheless, a refuge of peace where the country sounds of farmyard and field accentuate the calm; where a quick flash of amber amidst the greenery and shadows shows that the fox may still run despite his mortal enemy, man; where the faithful robin all but bursts his tiny heart in joyful song; where the barn owl may still be seen at dusk in graceful, ghostly flight.

It is here, also, that one may sometimes be surprised to hear the crackling bursts of a Rolls Royce *Merlin* coming to life. Occasionally, even, its unmistakable, steady bellow as it lifts a *Spitfire* into the air. And that, too, seems right and proper—for it was amongst such surroundings, fifty years ago, that the same sounds were heard, and the same turf was ruffled by slipstream, as the young men of Fighter Command bounded over the meadows to rise in defence of their homeland.

How is it, then, that the pleasant, unspoiled peace of the English countryside has apparently become enmeshed in a time warp of half a century ago?

It is because a remarkable man called Charles Church, who had made Micheldever his home, for a brief period of a busy life had a vision which compelled him to recreate history. Not content merely to read about it in books, or listen to tales of yesterday's airmen grown old in their memories, he determined to step into the past, to personally savour the sights, sounds and sensations of years ago.

It was here, amongst the gently rolling hills of Hampshire, at his own front door, that he established the means of living his dream.

In his contemporary world Charles was, in other ways, a shining example of the band of achievers who blazed trails of success through the years of opportunity which followed World War 2. No privileged landed aristocrat, he was a product of good, industrious middle-class English stock. With exactly the same opportunities and obstacles as countless other youngsters maturing in the post-war world, he quietly and diligently pulled ahead of the pack.

As his achievements indicate, Charles Church had plenty of ambition, but not in the avaricious, rather belligerent mould regrettably so prevalent today. His ambition was pitched at a higher level — to do his best for his family; to care for and help those with whom he worked and shared his daily life; to appreciate the environment in which we all live. Wealth, the reward of diligence, commercial acumen and courage, came his way, but it was always a means to an end. It presented the opportunity to improve the quality of life, not only for himself and his family, but for many thousands of home-seekers who benefitted from his flare and industry.

Charles Church achieved an enormous amount in a relatively short time. He was not merely a property developer. He developed property development. His was no opportunistic "...there's a bit of ground — let's build a house on it," type of activity. Looking at the results of his industry and vision it is clear that this quiet, thoughtful man had set out to provide quality housing, in quantity, for discerning people, in the right places for the right prices. Occupants who are fortunate enough to occupy those properties on the perimeter of London will testify that Charles Church achieved those aims entirely.

But that is another story in its own right. The aim of this narrative is to describe a different aspect of his life.

It is difficult to say when Charles first felt the urge to get personally involved in the business of regenerating veteran aircraft. It may have been that, like many a youth brought up in the shadows of war, he assumed an instinctive enthusiasm for the graceful and dashing machines of the '40s, and also for those of a slightly older generation who were privileged to operate them.

Charles Church's motivation may have been strong, but not, apparently, in the sense that he yearned to be a professional aviator. Had that been the case there was nothing, as far as one can see, to prevent him from so doing. His drive stemmed more from his desire to see for himself whether the business of flying high performance piston-engined fighters was really the adventure he had imagined it to be as a boy.

As a man, he clearly needed the stimulus of personal challenges. At some time in his life he had developed the interest, and good fortune and hard work had provided him with the means to satisfy his curiosity. It was not simply a matter of learning to fly by purchasing an aeroplane 'off the shelf'. That would have been far too tame. It all went far beyond that. It had to be a *Spitfire*, and, if possible, one in need of resuscitation to bring it back to life.

Charles Church decided that he would seek such a veteran aircraft, (or what was left of one), restore what was possible, replace what was not, or was missing, and get it back into the air, where it belonged.

When Charles began his search there were many others similarly engaged—for a variety of motives. Some were driven to exercise their engineering skills; some because the detective work involved in searching for the remains of old aircraft is attractive in itself; others for the challenge of flying aircraft which had been built before they were born; and yet more—a few—for purely mercenary reasons.

In the latter respect, it is ironical that at the war's end quite a number of people made instant fortunes by buying unwanted aircraft at knock-down prices in order to turn them into scrap, but by the '60s and '70s the tide had turned completely, with others making

Spitfires Reborn

money by buying scrap at knock-down prices and turning it into aircraft.

The acquisition of greater wealth in that fashion was never Charles Church's aim. Naturally, as a businessman of the highest standards it is understandable that he would have been keen to see that the organisation which emerged as a result of his enthusiasm would be properly regulated in every respect, including, if possible, financial self-sufficiency. But the business of Charles Church (*Spitfires*) Ltd. was to recreate *Spitfires*.

But without a professional aviation engineering background or, indeed, the time to carry out such a project, how was it to be done? How to get started?

It was that great Victorian cook, Mrs Beeton, who was reputed to have said, in relation to Bear Soup: "First, find yourself a bear." Charles Church followed a somewhat similar line by scanning the vintage aviation scene to try to discern what might be available in the pre-restoration category, which could possibly be turned back into a flyer.

It was not long before the opportunity to indulge his ambition presented itself. He already had at his disposal a pleasant stretch of Hampshire large enough to provide a grass landing strip and aircraft movement area. There was also space to accommodate a workshop-cum-hangar. There were some bits and pieces available which had once been a *Spitfire* which he thought could become one again.

So he was well on the way — and there we will leave him for the moment, pondering quietly on his next move.

Elsewhere in the vintage aviation industry (for that is what it had become) was another, very different personality who was destined to play a significant part in the Charles Church story. His name is Dick Melton.

Dick is a small, sprightly man, loquacious with a streak of wicked humour, and a fund of readily-stated opinions. Of indeterminate years, he is happily married to his wife and business partner, Carol. His other great love is his volcano of a pipe which accompanies him everywhere, and is put to work whenever circumstances allow. Dick is industrious and enthusiastic, and one quickly establishes the opinion that his work as an aviation engineer is at the same time his hobby.

His life in aviation was well-founded. As a boy, he did all he could to hang around the fringes of that world and, by so doing, fed his appetite for matters aeronautical and, indeed, his knowledge. As soon as he reached the qualifying age he donned RAF blue to become a 'Trenchard Brat' – an aircraft apprentice at the School of Technical Training at RAF Halton in Buckinghamshire.

Despite the rigours and strict discipline meted out by that establishment – or because of it – Dick shares the widespread view that there is no finer training in every respect than that afforded by Halton. He remains to this day immensely and rightly proud of having graduated from that institution.

His sense of pride and achievement is thoroughly understandable. Through the years, Halton has fulfilled its task of building and maintaining levels of technical excellence within the RAF in a manner unrivalled by any other similar organisation elsewhere in the world. At the same time, it has developed standards of physical fitness and character-building in young people to which few schools and colleges could aspire.

The rigours of Halton safely negotiated, Dick entered the larger world of RAF service, in those days, worldwide. He was soon to discover the aptness of that description. If a desire to travel was in one's nature, Transport Command of the Royal Air Force could not be bettered. At one time or another, Dick could find himself working in the burning, dry heat and grit of Aden, the dripping humidity of Singapore, or the biting cold of Newfoundland. He worked on pure jets, such as the decorous *Comets* and the suave *VC 10s*, the sturdy weight-lifting *C-130 Hercules* prop-jets and the last of the great pistons, the *Blackburn Beverley*, forcing its chunky shape through the atmosphere against all odds, powered by its four *Bristol Centaurus* engines.

Dick learned about running repairs 'down the route' and the oft-used red line entries – the logging of problems which would not prevent the aircraft from completing its task safely, but would need to be attended to on its return to base. From time to time Dick and his fellow technicians would willingly work overtime to lend a helping hand to civilian operators who may have run into difficulties. He says, in his sardonic way, that Transport Command, as it then was, claimed one's absolute loyalty for every hour of five years. Whatever one's personal circumstances, old or young, happy or morose, married or single, one's first priority was the business of supporting the RAF's front line without fail. In short, Dick Melton was proud to become, in service parlance, a Transport Aircraft Servicing Specialist — a TASSman.

It is necessary to have personally experienced service life to understand the sense of satisfaction engendered by its comradeship and mutual trust. It is a matter of total incomprehension to the majority of British people that there exists a small element of their fellow-countrymen and women who are willing to pack their 'small kits' at a moments notice, and without question, leave their loved ones, go anywhere, work and live in great discomfort and, sometimes, danger, for nothing more than the pride of accomplishment. But to a serviceman or woman there is no greater reward

After the varied experience of Transport Command, Dick Melton turned up in the south-west of England at RAF Chivenor and RAF St Mawgan. There he added the *Hawker Hunter*, the *Avro Shackleton* and the *Nimrod* to his list of aircraft types.

Then, life took a completely different turn for the Meltons. The attraction of working with historic aircraft drew him to RAF Coltishall and the Battle of Britain Flight. It was there that a good technician could exercise and enjoy all the practical skills to which Dick had been introduced in his youth at Halton, and from which he would eventually glean so much satisfaction. His appointment as the Flight's senior engineer lasted for the following nine years, and proved to be his last in the service of the RAF.

It also provided the foundation for a second career as a civilian which occupies him to this day. Dick decided that he should consolidate his varied experience provided by his service life by becoming a licensed engineer.

In recognition of the unusual nature and demands of life with the colours, the three services offer their retiring men and women so-called resettlement courses in certain general areas such as home and vehicle maintenance, business administration and the like. Such courses are undemanding, relaxed, and usually much enjoyed by the 'students' taking part, representative of all ranks from airman to most

The Micheldever Story

senior officer. The achievement of higher qualifications such as a commercial pilot's licence or, in Dick's case, an aircraft engineer's certificate, have to be financed by the individual.

However satisfying service life may be, it is not noted for lining the pockets of its loyal and industrious servants. After many years of uncomplaining and usually turbulent service one finds oneself, one day, standing with a suitcase, clearance chit and railway voucher outside the main gate. Just over the fence, one's erstwhile chums carry on about their lawful occasions (which had also been one's own until the day before), and keeping the flag flying high. They're still secure 'in the mob', and happy to be of service.

You, on the other hand, are not. You're out. Out in a world where your civilian counterparts have been beavering away at this and that occupation for all the years you have spent gamely sweating it out in the tropics, or freezing into insensibility on some windswept airfield in Europe or East Anglia.

What, then, is to be done?

In Dick and Carol's case they decided to go into the guest-house business. So, off they went to Dawlish, Devonshire, to invest their end-of-service gratuity in the purchase of an old Victorian house which would suit their purpose.

With negotiations proceeding, but needing something more positive to do, Dick took on some work for West Country Air Services at nearby Exeter. There he was able to exercise a relatively rare skill for the times—working with fabric. (The company was still accepting contracts for the repair of *Dakota* control surfaces).

Having almost accidentally entered the world of civil aviation, and despite the avowed intention of becoming a catering entrepreneur, Dick heard that Short Brothers were looking for someone with *Gipsy* engine experience to work on *Chipmunks* at West Malling, near Maidstone, Kent. He was offered the post, accepted it, abandoned all thoughts of making his fortune by producing full English breakfasts, and moved to Kent.

But not for long. Just thirteen months later all contracts came to an end with Short Brothers move to Northern Ireland in the offing. Once again, Dick Melton was out of a job.

There is a man of considerable reputation in the world of British vintage aviation. Doug Arnold, a wartime pilot, founded a company

Spitfires Reborn

called Warbirds of Great Britain at Blackbushe, Hampshire. One of the pioneers in the post-war emergence of this specialist activity, his company has worked on a global basis and is now arguably one of the most experienced and successful anywhere in the world.

Dick Melton, with his extensive track record with the Battle of Britain Flight, would clearly be of interest to Arnold. After the Short Brothers disappointment Dick offered his services, and there started an association which was mutually fruitful, and destined to continue for over five years.

It was a very active association. In his search for the remains of World War 2 aircraft Dick Melton and his boss followed the trail in many parts of the world, including Canada, Israel, India and, of course, Europe. Amongst other things, he worked on the restoration of a *P.47 Thunderbolt*, and a hybrid *Hurricane* with fuselage from Israel and wings from India. There were *Spitfires*, ex-Spanish *Hispano Buchons* (a licence-built *Me 109* with a *Merlin* engine), *CASA 352L (Junkers 52/3)*, and *CASA 2.111 (Heinkel 111* also with *Merlins*).

Notably, there was an extensive and difficult rebuild of a rare *Westland Lysander*. Indeed, that aeroplane provided a new experience for Dick Melton in more ways than one.

When flying as passenger en route to an airshow at Halfpenny Green the engine decided that it had done enough, and suffered a complete cut. The aircraft was flying at about 1,000 feet above ground level at the time. Warwickshire — beautiful county though it is — is not noted for wide expanses of flat, uncluttered land. The *Lysander*, for its part, was not designed to be able to cover much ground under conditions of zero power with a windmilling propeller. The combination of these factors left the pilot next to no choice when it came to picking a landing area. Indeed, the only practical proposition was a field where the corn had been harvested, and the stubble subsequently burnt. He made no misjudgment on the approach, floated nicely over the hedge and touched down neatly. Unfortunately, the port wheel dug into a depression which caused the aircraft to flip over on to its back. The good news was that both occupants emerged none the worse for that rather unnerving experience.

Dick Melton's time with the Battle of Britain Flight, and his subsequent experience as a civilian had made him into something of a paragon amongst the growing band of engineers specialising in veteran aircraft.

He had for some time had it in mind to adopt a more independent stance in this burgeoning business, and it seemed to him now that the sooner he did so the better.

After leaving the Doug Arnold camp, Dick freelanced for eighteen months or so as a consultant engineer. It was during that period that he met and worked with Nick Grace at St Merryn. This independent mode of life became very much to his liking and, indeed, was thoroughly attuned to his personality and background. He took a conscious decision that his name would never feature on any other business payroll again.

Now we must return to Charles Church, cogitating on his way ahead. In 1985 he happened to meet Dick Melton and, to his surprise, Charles invited him to help with the rebuild of a *Spitfire* to flying standard. It turned out to be *TE517*, a one-time plaything of Israeli children rescued from a kibbutz.

The job, of course, was tailor-made for Dick Melton—but first he was at pains to make his independent position quite clear. It was a proviso which Charles Church understood and sympathised with entirely. The result was that the two formally agreed that a contract should be drawn up relating to the rebuilding of one *Spitfire*.

At about that time Charles Church acquired what was left of a *Spitfire HF IX, PT462*. That, too, had been rescued from Israel in 1982 to be brought back to a temporary resting place at Fowlmere, Cambridgeshire. In fact, it really only amounted to a much deteriorated fuselage. That meant that a great deal of advanced work would be needed to fabricate an entirely new rear fuselage, the tail assembly and both mainplanes. Under the circumstances Charles Church decided that a conversion to a two-seater might just as well be undertaken at the same time.

Dick Melton settled easily into his new working environment—happy with the project and, above all, happy in the working relationship he now enjoyed with Charles Church, "...one of the very few nice guys in vintage aviation," says Dick. "Most of the others want service for nothing. They don't seem to realise that people like me are highly specialised in the very small field in which I operate. I

Spitfires Reborn

PT 462 (Chivers)

don't know anything other than the vintage aircraft business. People believe that you are only in it because you're a caring, kindly chap who wants nothing more than to lovingly bring old aeroplanes back to life. That's where you get your reward, in the satisfaction of doing so. So you don't need any pay. Well, I don't altogether go along with that philosophy."

Charles Church's motivation was unquestionable in both strength and sincerity. He was in it because of his desire to reproduce those famous 'planes of the past. He wanted today's generations to savour at least a taste of the atmosphere of a war which has passed into history so that, for a few brief moments they could get an inkling of the sights and sounds which changed the lives of their grandparents and parents.

Work went ahead. A hangar and workshop sprung up from a clearing in a copse on the Roundwood estate. More aircraft and components were added to the string — a *P 51 Mustang*, an *Hispano Buchon*, and a *Pilatus* bedecked with black crosses and swastika.

The tattered fuselage of *PT462* was the first to occupy the jig at Roundwood. Whilst Dick Melton and his assistants began the lengthy process of drilling out corroded rivets and repairing or replacing damaged metal, Trent Engineering at Castle Donnington, Leicestershire, set to work to construct a set of wings while Air Repair of Bicester, Oxfordshire, made headway with a new tail unit.

As a result of all this industry *PT462*, now modified to a *Type 509 Spitfire T.9* two-seater was the first to roll out of the workshop. After being successfully tested by John Lewis she stood ready to join the airshow circuit.

By now, yet more *Spitfire* relics were being located in various parts of the world. Harry van der Meer, the well-known Dutch *Spitfire* historian and enthusiast passed the news to Charles Church of the presence of another *Spitfire Mk IX* which had been used for many years as a training airframe at Fokker's apprentices' school, and then at a technical college. In this case, much had gone astray, including the wings. Dick Melton suspects that it was gradually being disposed of at the nearby scrap-metal yard. What was left was sold to Charles. Dick journeyed to the Nederlands to arrange for its movement. In the event, he managed part of that operation himself. He reports that he brought the forward bulkhead back to England as his personal baggage.

Other *Spitfire* components from a number of sources, including Australia, arrived at Roundwood to swell the Church collection. By 1988, everything had developed so quickly and successfully that Charles was giving much thought to the future management structure. In addition to the rebuilds already under way, the organisation had by now acquired a *Fairey Battle*, a badly damaged *Lancaster* and a partially restored *Hurricane* in addition to the *P 51, Buchon, Pilatus* and *PT462*, all of which were now available for airshows, film work and the like.

Dick Melton, despite the fact that his original contract had specified a single rebuild of a *Spitfire*, had already become involved in a much more diverse operation. He had, nevertheless, not changed his mind about his wish to remain master of his own fate.

Eventually, after deep consideration by Charles and Dick a solution was evolved to the satisfaction of all concerned. Whilst the collection and the real estate would, of course, remain under the control of Charles Church, Dick Melton Aviation would be formed as contractors to rebuild, maintain and operate the entire fleet. It would also be permitted to accept other commissions on an opportunity basis.

Spitfires Reborn

Whilst all that managerial activity was proceeding, work had started on the ex-Dutch *Mk IX PL344* and a *Spitfire Mk V* with the civil registration *G-MKVC*, based on components which had been obtained from Australia.

PL 344 (Chivers)

There are very few *Spitfire Mk Vs* in existence. Whilst this latter aircraft was virtually being recreated by Dick Melton only two other examples were flyable in the United Kingdom — *AB910* of the Battle of Britain Memorial Flight (as it had now become) and the highly authentic *AR501*, a much-valued item in the Shuttleworth Collection. Much interest, therefore, was centred on *G-MKVC*. That was enhanced when the aircraft had been completed, as it appeared in public wearing the identification letters of the late Gp. Capt. Sir Douglas Bader.

Saturday, 1st July.
A pleasant summer's morning full of promise for the flying planned for that day, which was also scheduled to mark the founding of Dick Melton Aviation.

Already rolled out on to the forecourt of the hangar stood the *Spitfire Mk V*, pristine and glinting in the morning sun. She was waiting to display her beauty at an airshow to be held that day at the British Aerospace airfield at Dunsfold.

Her pilot for the day, Flight Lieutenant David Southwood, was a qualified test pilot based at Boscombe Down, near Salisbury. David is one of today's highly skilled fast jet experts who, after a week's work with today's 'heavy metal', enjoys nothing more than to volunteer his services to fly yesterday's aircraft, to savour an earlier approach to the art of fighter flying.

By late morning David had taken off to carry out a little continuation training in order to re-acclimatise himself to the different, but quite demanding, requirements of this mount of another era. He posed the *Mk V* for a few minutes of video filming, after which he set course for Dunsfold.

Once there, David spent his Saturday off by carrying out two displays interspersed by some three hours on the ground, answering the awed questions of small boys, and, no doubt, listening tactfully to the rambling reminiscences of an earlier — much earlier — generation.

David Southwood had returned to Micheldever by tea-time, and handed the aircraft over to Dick Melton for refuelling and a 'turn-round' check. He then left the pleasant rural scene to do whatever test pilots do on a Saturday evening.

Charles Church, always striving to improve his flying techniques, had decided that he would take advantage of the lovely summer's evening to try to polish up his loops which he considered rather less than perfect. He was, by this time, fully familiar with this relatively recent addition to his stable, having flown it frequently during its twenty-seven hours of flying life. Charles was, in any event, quite an experienced pilot in comparison with many wartime *Spitfire* pilots, with well over five hundred hours to his credit.

It is not fitting that this part of the narrative should be prolonged. It is only necessary to relate that, about half-an-hour after take-off the engine of that beautifully restored aircraft suffered a catastrophic failure. The pilot did all he could under such circumstances by sending clear 'Mayday' calls over the radio, and setting up the conditions for a forced landing.

All was to no avail. A few minutes later *G-MKVC* was destroyed, taking her pilot with her. The quiet, determined, likeable man, who had always wanted to fly a *Spitfire*, had been deserted by the fortune

Spitfires Reborn

which had previously favoured him so well, at the very moment that it was most needed.

In the shadow of such tragedy it may be thought that the cares and disappointments of others fade into total insignificance. That is not necessarily the case.

Dick and Carol Melton's first thoughts, without a doubt, were for the immediate family of Charles Church. But there must have been created in his own mind such turmoil as called for every last atom of self-discipline as he possessed to preserve a constructive balance.

First there was the warm personal relationship which the two men had enjoyed. Second, he needed to accept the fact that it was the aircraft on which he had lavished so much time and effort which had been the instrument of the tragedy. Of course, the circumstances were totally beyond the control of any human agency — but who thinks of that at such a time? Third, 1st July was the very day chosen to usher Dick Melton Aviation on to the vintage aviation scene in its own right. Lastly, his band of technical assistants had chosen that day to move off to pastures new.

To Dick and Carol it must have been Black Saturday indeed. But people who have lived many years of their lives under service conditions have been brought up to expect and accept adversity from time to time; to learn to 'get off their knees' when things go wrong; and to recognise that there are times when there is nowhere to go but up.

Dick and Carol Melton, like the Londoners of the Blitz, had learned how to take it.

The aftermath of personal tragedy is always unspeakably hard. When it concerns one who, in all too short a life, had made such an impact in both his personal and professional relationships, and whose potential was still largely untapped, the shock to those nearest and dearest to him can scarcely be imagined.

With great calmness and bravery Mrs Susannah Church decided, quite quickly, that her husband's policies, so recently arrived at, should remain. She was, and is, determined that, as far as she is able, Charles' aviation interests will continue as a fitting tribute to him, and as a constant reminder of his efforts to see that this country's aviation heritage is not taken for granted.

The Micheldever Story

More Micheldever Spitfires undergoing restoration in the hands of Dick melton's team. Top is SM832, bottom is TE 517 (Chivers)

Dick Melton is not the man to sink without a fight. Dick Melton Aviation is a reality, and living at Micheldever. His work force has been rebuilt, mainly by the recruitment of ex-servicemen with whom, of course, he is very much at home. And there is plenty for them to do.

Spitfires Reborn

The ex-Dutch *Spitfire Mk IX PR344*, denizen of training schools, provider of scrap, some-time the personal baggage of Dick Melton, took to the air again early in 1991. The intention was always to offer a *Mk IX* for sale in order to help fund the continuing operation. That will be done in due course.

So, if at any time you are passing along the leafy lanes of Hampshire, in the vicinity of the English village of Micheldever, and above the purring of your car you hear the unmistakable bellow of a Rolls Royce *Merlin* under take-off power, pause to think of that classic fighter of fifty years ago to which this country owes so much.

At the same time, think of Charles Church, the man who had the vision to bring his *Spitfire* back to life, and who fulfilled his boyhood dream by flying it.

MV 297 coming together at Micheldever. (Chivers)

Oh ... and *Spitfire TE517*? The ex-Czech, ex-Israeli wreck which was rescued from a children's playground in a kibbutz, and for which Dick Melton was contracted by Charles Church to make flyable?

It's still a restored fuselage at the back of the hangar — the last in the queue. But never fear, Susannah Church and Dick Melton will put her back one day, in the place where she belongs, in the air.

CHAPTER SIX
Spitfires and Saviours

Unlike its wartime companion, the *Hawker Hurricane*, every one of the 22,500 *Spitfires* were made in England. Many of them travelled far, both during and after the war. Indeed, at one time or another, *Spitfires* in varying numbers became the property of no less than thirty-three nations. Wherever they ended up, whether in their home country or in 'some corner of a foreign field' 99% became derelict or reduced to scrap. Some were merely pushed to one side and left to rot; a few were more or less stripped internally and raised on plinths as monuments to the past; one or two found their ways into museums to be preserved as historic relics, others, the less fortunate, became the playthings of children alongside the swings and see-saws in their playgrounds.

Their travelling days were not — are not — necessarily over. During recent years there has arisen a growing interest worldwide in old aircraft and their preservation. This has been partly due to an academic desire to maintain tangible links with the past; also, there has been a phenomenal rise in interest by the general public in the entertainment value of air displays, some of which have reached extraordinary heights of pageantry. With this increased stimulation there has grown the realisation that almost anything can be resurrected.

Whatever political motivation exists amongst our fellow nations, we live undeniably in a world of supply and demand. In terms of

Spitfires Reborn

collectable aircraft the *Spitfire* is at the same time rare and pre-eminent. It is therefore at the top of the collectors' market; the world's few remaining examples of surviving airframes, (as far as is known), in whatever state of dilapidation, are prime targets for restorers.

The natural consequence of this state of affairs is that an air of extreme secretiveness, matched only by the shadowy world of espionage, pervades the business of tracking down and securing the remaining bits of battered hardware.

A slightly more open environment exists in the wheeling and dealing concerned with *Spitfires* and components which have already been secured by civilian owners. 'Slightly', because even in that circle there have been odd mysteries arising from time to time. But in general it is true to say that all in the business know who's got what, in what condition and status, and whether or not there's likely to be any trading in the offing. Thus, there are private deals to be struck, either on a cash basis, or involving swaps. In addition, the trade has attracted the attention of the elite of dealers such as Christie's and Sotheby's.

The market is active and worldwide. Consequently, pieces of *Spitfire* — or any other historic aircraft for that matter — from single manufacturer's data plates to whole aircraft are constantly on the move. *Spitfires* by the hundreds left their native shores long ago. Some of the remnants have been sought out, tenderly boxed, and brought back to be painstakingly renovated. Some, in far fewer numbers, have returned to foreign shores where they are enjoyed and much admired. One thing is certain. Wherever they go they will receive the attention due to thoroughbreds from people who value them. As one of my friends once remarked : "Nobody really owns a *Spitfire*. They just pay for the privilege of looking after it for a few years."

Let us take a closer look at some of today's civilian 'minders' and the stories behind their acquisitions.

THE SHUTTLEWORTH COLLECTION

The story of the Shuttleworth Collection really began with Richard Ormond Shuttleworth. He was born in 1909, the son of a prosperous Bedfordshire landowner. For one privileged to be born into such circumstances his upbringing was wholly appropriate to the heir apparent of the mature and delightful lands set amongst the gently undulating fields and woodlands of the area.

From infancy the boy was brought up in the best traditions of the responsible English squire, wherein the title to lands carried with it unbreakable obligations towards tenants and estate residents, personal management, and the encouragement of good husbandry.

As he grew towards maturity and the appointed time when he would inherit the estates in his twenty-third year, he became deeply interested and personally involved in motor sports and flying. Richard drove successfully at Brooklands and Castle Donnington (the great motor racing tracks of the day), and took part in most of the principal Continental meetings.

He had gained his Private Pilot's Licence before he had reached the age of twenty years, a move which enabled him to purchase his first aeroplane, a *de Havilland 60X Hermes Moth*. Amongst other things, Richard used it to ease the commuting problem between Old Warden and the racing circuits. Remarkably, that seventy years old aircraft still exists and may be seen at Old Warden Open Days.

Arising from his interests in flying, Shuttleworth met and befriended George Stead, a serving officer of the RAF. In 1933 they made a noteworthy flight, in company, to India to take part in the Viceroy's Challenge Trophy race. Their mounts for that marathon journey were *Comper Swifts*, tiny open cockpit sports monoplanes.

Richard's interests in aviation were all-embracing. He formed the Warden Aviation Company which chartered and hired out a *de Havilland Dragon*, three *Comper Swifts*, three *Desoutters* and his own *DH 60X*. The aircraft were maintained at Old Warden but operated out of Heston (today all but lost in the sprawl of Heathrow). He also took an active interest in an emerging enterprise of the day when he formed his company Aeronautical Advertising Ltd. which used

Spitfires Reborn

smoke trails and neon lettering. He was, at the same time, a working Director of Comper Aircraft Company. It is difficult to understand how Richard Shuttleworth found the time to run the estates, but find it he did; he was, in fact, very popular with his tenants and staff, and an extremely effective manager.

During 1935 Richard became interested in a civic project aimed at building an airport for Bedford. It was during that year that he happened to meet a local garage owner, A E Grimmer, of Ampthill. That gentleman had preserved what, even for those days, were two great rarities, a *Bleriot Type XI* monoplane and a *Deperdussin* of 1910 vintage. Both machines were acquired by Richard Shuttleworth, and so marked the beginning of one of the world's first collections of veteran aircraft.

By 1939 the Shuttleworth Collection of old cars and aeroplanes had grown considerably. It was (and is) housed within the estate on a small, grassy field which provides exactly the right atmosphere for the aircraft which are now exhibited on a regular monthly basis.

Old Warden is one of those rare places which requires a peaceful drive through leafy, country by-roads. One comes upon it almost by surprise, tucked away as it is between mature woodland copses. Eventually, one turns off the road to bump across sweet-smelling meadow grass to park the car before walking along the line of beautifully preserved old aircraft. As they stand silent at their chocks, with the smell of freshly mown grass in one's nostrils, one becomes aware of the merest hum of the summer breeze wafting gently through the wires and struts of the biplanes. It is easy for anyone with a sense of history or, for the older observer actual memories, to be transported back over the years to another world of half a century ago.

War came to Old Warden, just as it did throughout the whole of Europe, on 3rd September, 1939. The little airfield was 'called up' for war work, occupied by Shrager Bros. Ltd., who had been contracted to service the RAF's trainers, *Tiger Moths* and *Miles Magisters*. The fleets of old vehicles and veteran aircraft were carefully inhibited and put into safe storage for the duration of the war.

Richard Shuttleworth, with plenty of flying experience behind him, and with a high level of technical knowledge, signed up in the Royal Air Force Volunteer Reserve, as did all other volunteers who joined up after war had been declared. Sadly, the cruellest fate took a hand. Richard Shuttleworth, having just completed his operational training in 1940, was killed whilst night flying in a *Fairey Battle*.

Some four years later, Shuttleworth's mother founded a trust which today preserves the memory of her son whose brief life of just thirty-one years had been so eventful and constructive. Today, the Shuttleworth Trust directs the affairs of the Agricultural College and the Collection of old vehicles and aircraft.

Today, visitors to Old Warden are guaranteed a feast of aviation nostalgia and historical interest. Up to thirty different aircraft types may be present, most of them in flying condition. Some are now unique in the world.

In addition to Shuttleworth's indigenous collection, veteran aircraft from elsewhere are often invited to take part. The Battle of Britain Memorial Flight frequently puts in an appearance when flying to and from other events. It is back to the age of pistons and propellers. The only jets normally to be heard are the airliners going about their lawful occasions six miles above.

Standing with its somewhat older brethren there will almost certainly be *Spitfire Mk LF VC AR501*. This is probably one of the most authentic examples of her vintage. The purists will be quick to notice the three-bladed airscrew, the correct radio aerial and the reflector gunsight mounted before the pilot's eyes behind the laminated windscreen.

How has this long-lived fighter managed to survive the years?

AR501 was built by Westland Aircraft under contract, joining the RAF on 22nd June, 1942. The aircraft was delivered to No 310 (Czech) Squadron, then at Exeter, on 19th July, 1942. About nine months later she was damaged in a flying accident which necessitated her return to No 67 Maintenance Unit, Taunton, for repairs.

By the time they were completed (3rd July, 1943) the *Spitfire Mk V's* time was running out as far as front-line operations were concerned. *AR501* was shuffled to and from units without, apparently, too much thought being given to her long-term future. Staying weeks, or sometimes days, at a succession of units, *AR501* was eventually permitted to settle down for a while with No 61 Operational Training Unit.

Spitfires Reborn

By 9th September, 1944, she was once again back in the hands of the repairers—this time Air Service Training, Hamble. Her service life came to an end on 24th March, 1946 when she was sold to Loughborough College for use as an instructional airframe.

The aircraft remained in that capacity for 15 years, until such time as the technology employed in the construction of the *Spitfire* finally became outdated.

In 1961 *AR501* joined the Shuttleworth Collection in a dismantled state, and remained in that condition until 1967. It was then that she was dusted down and surveyed as a potential flyer for the film, 'The Battle of Britain'. Despite her twenty-two years on the ground she was quickly made airworthy again, in time to star in the film.

That glamorous task completed the aircraft was once again put into storage, this time at Thurleigh, where she remained for the next six years. In 1973 *AR501* was moved to Duxford. There, she was completely stripped to undergo a rebuild which was to take two years. She emerged fit for flying, to be test-flown by the late Neil Williams on 27th June, 1975. She remains airworthy to this day, much to the delight of her many fans.

PETER ARNOLD'S SEAFIRE

I am fortunate to number amongst my friends a man called Peter Arnold who lives at Newport Pagnell, a small town in Buckinghamshire. (Incidentally, there are a confusing number of Arnolds in the vintage aircraft world, so I should make it clear that Peter and Doug Arnold have no family connections whatsoever).

Peter is, in my opinion and that of many others, the most authoritative voice to be heard in today's *Spitfire* world. His background knowledge comes as a result of an admiration for the aircraft which has developed since childhood, and his own engineering skills and technical understanding which underpin his earlier subjective assessment.

It is a remarkable fact that, although a highly skilled engineer in the automotive industry, Peter Arnold has had no professional connection with aircraft engineering either civilian or with the military. I called on him recently to find out more about him and his unusual restoration project.

"It all started when I was a kid," he told me. "I was born on 3rd December, 1941, a few days before Pearl Harbour. In the early fifties I went to school at the County Grammar School, Harrow. That's the one at the bottom of the Hill," he explained. "Incidentally, that was the school that educated John Boothman, the Schneider Trophy pilot. At the main entrance we had a big stained-glass window in commemoration of the Schneider Trophy victory. That used to attract my attention a lot. Well, some kids collect railway engine numbers, some get interested in old cars and motorbikes. I got hooked on second World War aircraft — and the *Spitfire* in particular."

When schooldays were over Peter decided to develop his interest in engineering by entering the motor industry. Life was very busy as he worked to widen his experience; the hobby of his younger days fell to a lowly position in his list of life's priorities, and stayed so as family matters and work left little time or energy to think of anything else.

His early interest in the *Spitfire* may have been dormant for a while, but it did not leave him altogether. If it was to become anything at all, however, Peter knew enough about himself to realise that a mere academic study of the aircraft would fail to satisfy him. Somehow or other he would eventually need to get actively involved with the hardware. But, unlike a number of activists in the business of aircraft preservation, Arnold had not been born with a silver spoon in his mouth, so it was difficult to accept the possibility of making much headway.

The chance came, however, in 1971 when the opportunity presented itself for Peter Arnold and a friend, Neville Franklin to jointly acquire the remains of two *Seafire* fuselages from Bill Francis of Southend. Peter became sole owner two years later by which time he had uncovered two more cockpit sections and fuselages from a scrapyard in Warrington, plus wings and two *Griffon* engines. He was not able to acquire the wings as they had already been sold, but Peter was able to make an arrangement with his partner Neville Franklin whereby he would become sole owner of the original fuselages which, together with the remainder of the Warrington scrap, would significantly increase his collection. Indeed, that pile of 'worthless' scrap was destined to become metamorphosised over the years into a *Seafire F.46, LA564*.

The story to date is one of twenty years of dedication, patient and intelligent manoeuvring in the world of vintage aircraft, developing new engineering skills, and a lot of hard work. It has not been easy.

In order to understand why anyone can think it imperative to indulge in the sort of masochism which must be endured to remake a heap of rusting scrap into a sleek and gleaming aircraft it might be helpful to take a brief look at its history.

The *Seafire* was the naval version of the *Spitfire*. The penultimate version was the *Seafire F.46*, built at Castle Bromwich in 1945. Only twenty-four were completed; *LA564* was the last to come off the line. All were in component form, delivered to South Marston, Wiltshire for final assembly. The *Seafire 46* never reached the naval front line; some went to No 781 Training Squadron at Lee-on-Solent and some to No 1832 Squadron, Royal Navy Volunteer Reserve at Culham.

LA564 was delivered to the Receipt and Dispatch Unit at Anthorn only to be sold as scrap to Daniel Clark & Co., Carlisle. J D Kay of Manchester Tankers, Charnock Richard, Lancashire rescued what was left in 1966, where it remained for a further five years. It was then, in 1971, that Franklin and Arnold took possession. As we have seen, the partnership came to an amicable end in 1973 when both partners went in their own individual directions.

Once having taken over his own project, Peter Arnold was faced with the dilemma of how to proceed. The first barrier was lack of funds. The late '60s and early '70s were bad times throughout the country. Recession had plunged to its most dismal depths, unemployment had soared, redundancies were everyday occurrences. Peter and his wife, Kay were struggling through all this to bring up a young family. The proposition that hard-earned cash should be spent on an old *Seafire* was unthinkable.

Despite the problems, Peter did make progress. He described to me the extraordinary lengths to which he, and others, would go to keep up some sort of momentum. An example of the payment-in-kind manoeuvring which actually achieved results concerned a pair of *Seafire* outer wings which he needed, but were in the possession of Keith Fordyce, a keen collector. As such, his prime interest was concerned with getting patrons through the front door of his museum. Absolute authenticity came second.

When Peter Arnold stated his need for the genuine, if dilapidated *Seafire* outer wings, Fordyce was quite straightforward. He said: "Peter, times are hard. I'll not beat about the bush. The price for those wings is a full size replica glass-fibre *Spitfire* — and that's that."

That was a definite stumbling block. Peter knew, however, that other collectors had also shown an interest in those same outer wings, so it was necessary for him to close the deal. That was no simple matter as, in the end, it involved a chain of swaps with second, third and fourth parties and all sorts of different pieces of *Spitfire*, *Seafire* and fibre glass facsimiles. The details are too confusing and numerous to relate here. Suffice it to say that, because of his knowledge of other people's needs, Peter was able to work out this complicated scheme whereby everybody ended up happily with what they wanted in the way of swaps.

It was about that time that Peter decided to take a good look at what he'd got — rather in the manner of a boy fitting together a new plastic model. So he laid out the various components of his *Seafire* — over the front garden, into part of his neighbour's drive, over the pavement and into the road (happily, it was a cul-de-sac). This, fairly naturally, created a great deal of interest. In fact, it caused such a stir as to attract immediate media attention, first locally, then nationally, including BBC Television and ITV.

Peter decided that the right approach would be to get the business of publicity over in one big session. He sent out a press release which had the desired effect. It was a good story, favourable to Peter. On the day, to add a little style to the proceedings, Doug Arnold turned up in his helicopter with some more small items to add to the collection. Peter was interviewed and photographed with his exhibits, and he was given a seven-minute appearance on the Nationwide current events television programme.

The publicity assisted Peter in a number of ways. He discovered that various large organisations had become aware of his work and were quite prepared to take an interest. Rolls Royce at Leavesden took on the task of rebuilding the *Griffon* engine as an apprentices' learning vehicle. British Aerospace helped with the fin. At about the same time Frank Sanders, recently returned from Burma, where he had been looking for *Sea Fury* spares, dispatched a complete *Seafire XV* wing from California, via a third-party exchange.

The process of collecting and exchanging became an interest in itself. Peter discovered that the more one goes on, knowledge in addition to tangible components is stored away, and more doors open. At one time Peter had four tail units for various marks of *Spitfire*. One, originally from a *Mk XIV*, has been adapted for fitment to the fuselage of *LA564*. He was able to supply a number of components for a *Spitfire PR XIX* to the Royal Swedish Air Museum in exchange for which the Museum donated a propeller. Other pieces have been donated or swapped by the Royal Navy, the Canadian Warplane Heritage, the Belgian Air Force Museum, Scottish Aviation and the Royal Air Force.

Another result of the friendly publicity Peter had received was that he made the acquaintance of Bob Tattam. Bob was a batchelor who worked for British Aerospace at Hatfield. He was a general fitter, but was adept at practically everything to do with practical work on aircraft. One evening he telephoned Peter and asked if he could drop by to see for himself what was going on. Naturally, Peter concurred—and has never ceased to be pleased that he did so. All sorts of mysteries were made clear to him, and problems solved. Bob not only knew how to do things such as de-rivetting and re-rivetting, he was willing to teach Peter as he went along. Furthermore, he would take away pieces needing refurbishment to carry out the work in his bachelor flat. Bob was also knowledgeable about the type and source of supply of the various materials used in restoration work.

Eventually, Peter's collection became so extensive that he ran out of space, so he and Kay moved house to their present abode in Newport Pagnell which had the potential for an extension which he designed himself. He has installed all his aircraft material therein, and now that the years of work on the fuselage are behind him he finds that he can spend much more time in the home (the boys are now grown up). As time goes by Peter takes every opportunity to upgrade the quality of the project.

This enormous personal effort over many years has resulted in Peter gaining a vast fund of knowledge about today's *Spitfire* world. He has not wasted it. Every nugget of information is neatly filed and cross-referenced, every photograph properly referenced and captioned, every significant name and address registered. He is now, more than ever, in a position to help others as a reliable, trusted consultant with no axe to grind.

I asked him what plans he has for the future. He replied: "I'm not going to fly the aeroplane. That is not my interest. I will continue to search and collect wherever it may take me. The obsessive years of the 70s are over. I'm glad. They were hard years for all of us — and what gives me the greatest joy is that all of us in the family survived the strain. Now, the fact that we hung on to the project through thick and thin means the very presence of our aircraft provides us with the opportunity to travel abroad together on some missions."

A man with a mission — Peter Arnold in his workshop Newport Pagnell, 1991. (Arnold)

Peter has also started work on another rarity, a *Spitfire Mk XII*. A data plate on Frame 5 — the centre structure of all *Spitfires* has identified it positively as *EN224*. "Of course," he said as I admired his handiwork just before taking my leave, "simply because I said that I won't fly the aircraft, it is no longer my intention to see in them nothing but a grounded exhibit."

His eyes gleamed. "One day, maybe in the next ten years, I'm certain that these two aeroplanes will take to the air again."

Knowing Peter Arnold, I, too, am sure they will.

Spitfires Reborn

ELIMINATING THE IMPOSSIBLE

As Sherlock Holmes said to Dr Watson, "...when you have eliminated the impossible, whatever remains, however improbable, must be the truth."

On the Isle of Wight, divided by the Solent seaway from Southern Hampshire, Steve Vizard heads his own company with the apt and alliterative name Airframe Assemblies Limited. Steve's first attraction to aviation history was through the intricacies of aviation archaeology—to the layman, the business of tracking down old sites of aircraft crashes (or, occasionally, deliberate internment) prior to going on to the physically demanding exercise of attempting to recover whatever may be left in the vicinity either above or below ground.

That activity—research in the truest sense—develops a wide range of knowledge in those enthusiasts taking part. In most cases the prelude to pinpointing a site with the required accuracy means gleaning knowledge from combat reports or some other form of official documentation, from eye-witnesses (who are getting fewer in number as the years take their toll) or, perhaps, if the searcher is very fortunate, the pilot or aircrew member who survived to tell the tale. Then, assuming the selected site turns out to be accurate and starts to yield the evidence which has lain hidden for fifty years, the many bits and pieces which emerge must be properly identified. By that means a fund of technical knowledge is gradually built up about the systems, age and origin of the ill-fated aircraft.

Eventually Steve Vizard's interest became such that he decided to take the plunge by moving into the aviation business professionally. The vintage aviation industry had started to leap ahead by the late '70s, and there were (and still are) openings to be found for people whose asset is knowledge and whose motivation is enthusiasm. Steve was able to take advantage of such an opening by going to work for Aero Vintage Ltd., based at St Leonards-on-Sea.

The company was the brain-child of two well-known members of the veteran aircraft fraternity, Guy Black and Steve Atkins. Aero Vintage was engaged in the business of rebuilding aircraft; during the period of Steve Vizard's employment with the company, major work was being carried out on two *Spitfire Mk IXs, TE566* and *MJ730*, and a *Spitfire T.9, PV202*.

A quick glimpse at the histories of those aircraft reveals that the work which was carried on over the three years must have been basic rebuilding demanding the highest skills and advanced technical expertise. The two *Mk IXs* both had active but diverse histories. *TE566* disappeared into Czechoslovakia shortly after its emergence from Castle Bromwich, after which it re-appeared in Israel in 1949. It might just as well have remained behind the Iron Curtain for all that is known of its active service life with the Israeli Air Force. Once retired, it found its way to that graveyard of retired Israeli *Spitfires*, a kibbutz children's playground.

MJ730 was an older aeroplane which left Castle Bromwich in 1943. Like many of the same batch, she was crated and shipped to No 145 Maintenance Unit, Casablanca. There, she was re-assembled, air tested and delivered to No 249 Sqn., Middle East Air Forces. Once the fighting came to an end, and squadrons were disbanded or proceeded to their peacetime locations, many aircraft were disposed of locally. That was the case with *MJ730*, which was passed to the Italians. Once again, virtually nothing is known of its Italian service. It re-surfaced in Israel in 1950; it was simply found, derelict, at yet another kibbutz before being brought back to England.

Steve Vizard saw that *Spitfire* restorers—or, indeed, any vintage aircraft enthusiasts—are prepared, in the current climate of interest, to go to almost any lengths to fashion their own components whenever forced to do so. Why not, he reasoned, set up the industry's own provider? As it happens, there exists in the Isle of Wight, a resident pool of craftsmen which has formed over the years from the boatbuilding industry, followed later by the aircraft industry dating from Saunders-Roe, British Hovercraft, Westlands and Britten-Norman. That was where Steve Vizard made his first tentative entry into the business of component manufacture.

It is a measure of the market that Airframe Assemblies now produce panels and other parts for various *Spitfire* projects which are currently under way—over twenty at the last count. Now, the company is able to produce all types of rudders, elevators and ailerons over the *Spitfire* range. Furthermore, it can produce to order

Spitfires Reborn

radiator fairings, flaps, undercarriage doors—indeed, just about every description of skinning and fairing one could apply to a *Spitfire*.

It seems that it is now within the bounds of possibility to construct an entirely new *Spitfire* airframe from scratch. Properly powered by a *Merlin* or *Griffon* engine driving a Hoffman propeller, would such an aircraft be a replica, a facsimile, or a genuine *Spitfire*?

If one agrees with Conan Doyle, when the impossible has been eliminated, (genuine Vickers-Supermarine parts), whatever remains (newly manufactured components) must be the truth!

Spitfire Mk VIII MT719 A SEAC Veteran

Spitfire LF VIII MT719 (featured on the back cover) was built by Vickers-Armstrongs (Supermarine) and delivered in early 1944. It was one of 700 of the variant ordered, the majority of which were shipped directly to Australia or India. In the Far East a total of fifteen squadrons, including units of the RAAF, were equipped with *Mk VIIIs*.

The operational life of the *Spitfire Mk VIII* was not a long one. That was partly because it was late in coming off the production lines and, to some extent, the *Mk IX*, which was hurriedly introduced as an interim variant, filled the requirement adequately enough. By late 1944 the *Mk VIII* was generally being replaced by the *Griffon*-engined *Spitfire Mk XIV*. It was completely withdrawn from front line service by early 1946.

At that time 135 *Spitfire Mk VIIIs* serving with the RAF in Australia were transferred at no charge to the RAAF—a gift which was apparently not needed as the Australians themselves put 335 *Spitfires*, mostly *Mk VIIIs*, into long-term storage. It has been rumoured, but not substantiated, that a large number of these aircraft were consigned to a watery grave in the vicinity of the Great Barrier Reef.

MT719 escaped that fate. She arrived in Bombay on 5th September, 1944. The aircraft was allocated to No 17 Squadron, coded *YB-J*, and flown by 'B' Flight in operations against the Japanese until the unit left Burma in June 1945. At that time *MT719* was flown by Flt Lt Don Healey to Madura, India. There she apparently remained for more than two years before being handed over to the Indian Air Force on 29th December, 1947.

After that date there is no accurate record of the aircraft's use. It was said to have been used as a front-line aircraft for a while before being transferred to training duties. The only certainty is that *MT719* eventually ended up on a disused airfield at Jaipur.

In early 1977 the Indian Ministry of Defence announced that eight *Spitfires* were to be sold by auction. Ormond Hayden-Baillie who, with his brother Wensley had established their Aircraft and Naval Collection, flew out to India to inspect them all at their various locations. Their condition varied from 'very poor' to 'good'. *MT719*, the only *Mk VIII*, was said to be good—but such an assessment is in the eye of the beholder. Such photographs as are available show an aircraft in the open minus airscrew, canopy and, apparently, main wheels, controls unlocked, and with considerable damage to the skin of the port mainplane, wing root fairings and all flying control surfaces. Fortunately, the Rolls Royce *Merlin 66*, the propeller and spinner had been moved into the nearby hangar.

What a mess—Burma veteran MT719 Spitfire MK VIII as found in India.

Spitfires Reborn

The Hayden-Baillies made a successful bid against the opposition which included collectors from the USA.

Shortly after their return from India, Ormond Hayden-Baillie was killed flying a *P-51 Mustang* in Germany on 3rd July, 1977. Wensley had to arrange for the transfer of ownership before he was able to dispatch a team to see to the dismantling of all the aircraft, their packing and movement back to England. That was eventually achieved despite the fact that the locally manufactured crates were found to be too large for the containers available. There was no alternative but to unpack the aircraft and remake the crates. On arrival back in England the Executors had to be dispose of all the assets of the collection. That included, of course, *MT719*.

In Italy Franco Actis already owned a considerable fleet of flyable aircraft. It so happened that it had been a boyhood ambition to fly a *Spitfire* and he was quickly off the mark in securing the *Mk VIII* for himself. So, once again, *MT719* was crated and shipped off to Turin.

MT 719, as delivered to Italy, and following paint-stripping for inspection by her new owners.

The aircraft arrived in December 1980. Peter Arnold (see last chapter) advised that the six coats of old paint still remaining on the aircraft should be carefully stripped off, one by one. It was only by so doing that the RAF serial *MT719* was finally revealed, confirming that this was, indeed, the ex-17 Sqn. aircraft of thirty-five years ago.

The other consequence of stripping the paint was that the true state of the airframe was revealed for the first time. There were grave doubts concerning the likelihood of the aircraft ever flying again. British Aerospace in Italy carried out X-rays which showed up severe internal corrosion in the engine. Also, the port wing rear spar was almost eaten through by corrosion.

At this stage a former RAF technician, Paul Mercer, became involved to the extent that he decided to stay with the project as a full-time consultant. He was assisted when time would allow by two members of the Battle of Britain Memorial Flight, electrician 'Kick' Houltby and Pete Rushen. Paul discovered that the aircraft had at some time suffered a belly-landing sustaining damage which could only be rectified by reskinning. Additionally, it was deemed necessary to give both mainplanes similar treatment. Eventually, ninety per cent of the original magnesium rivets were replaced, and the whole structure was completely rewired.

Such deep surgery revealed some surprises. It was discovered that the manufacturer's part number showed that the starboard wing related to a *Spitfire Mk VII*. In fact, there were only minor differences in construction which clearly had no adverse effect on the aircraft's handling. An inspector's gauge and a small spanner set were also recovered after lying undetected for thirty-seven years.

The original *Merlin 66* was stripped down by Aermeccanica of Italy, and was found to have cracked cylinder heads and widespread corrosion. The Hayden-Baillie Collection produced a 1,740 hp *Merlin 114A* from a *Mosquito Mk 35* bomber which was modified and fitted to *MT719*.

By the summer of 1982 the aircraft had been finally assembled by Savoia-Marchetti, Milan. The engine was given its first post-restoration run on 25th August. Sqn. Ldr. Paul Day of the Battle of Britain Memorial Flight arrived in Italy in October and took MT719 (civilian registration I-SPIT) up on test flight on 17th October. On 30th October he flew the aircraft on the short hop to Malpensa where its

Spitfires Reborn

Spitfire MK VIII MT719 with three of its pilots. L to R: Flt. Lt. Don Healey, wartime pilot of this aircraft in the Burma campaign; Sqdn. Ldr. Paul Day, test pilot for this Spitfire and pilot for BBMF; Franco Actis, Spitfire pilot and, at the time, owner of the featured aircraft.

proud owner, Franco Actis, took it up for his first Spitfire solo flight. Thereafter, *MT719*, in her original South East Asia Command colours (apart from its civilian registration letters) was seen at numerous venues in Europe. In the summer of 1986 it returned to its home country to take part in the 50th *Spitfire* Anniversary display at the Army Air Corps Centre, Middle Wallop.

In 1989 ownership of *MT719* changed — Franco Actis having apparently sated his appetite for *Spitfire* flying. *Spitfire Mk VIII* has finally come home and is now in the hands of Adrian Reynard of Oxford (better known in the world of motor racing).

SPITFIRE MK V BL628 A RARE FIND

Not far from Andover, Hampshire is an airfield which is, itself, a survivor of World War 2. It is called Thruxton. It has somehow managed to remain in being, despite periods of gross neglect, while other historic aviation sites have withered and died. RAF Andover is a prime example of the latter.

In recent years, however, Thruxton seems to have become firmly established, partly because of its second activity, motor racing. There is also some very interesting aircraft restoration work going on there with what amounts to a production line of North American *AT 6s — Harvards* to the British. The company, which is a relative newcomer to the professional restoration scene (although its constituent members have long and successful track records) is called Aerofab. It is basically a partnership originally set up by David John and Tony Spooner who have previously been involved with both Dick Melton and Doug Arnold. Other members of the Aerofab team are Pat McLarry, Ian Browning, Peter Pykett and Steve Black.

Aerofab have recently rolled out a beautifully restored ex-Mozambique *Harvard* — one of six recovered from that distant land by John Woodhouse and Andrew Eadie. That aircraft having gone on its way, the dust sheets have been taken off a most interesting project — a *Spitfire Mk V BL628*, which will, it is hoped, one day grace the skies of Australia.

Spitfire Mk V BL628 was just one of 1,000 *Spitfire Mk IIIs* ordered from Castle Bromwich on 24th October, 1940. As was often the case with Spitfires, progressive improvements during construction were incorporated which enabled the total order to emerge as *Mk Vs*.

BL628 was given its first air test by the Chief Test Pilot at Castle Bromwich, Alex Henshaw, famous for his pre-war air racing and long distance record breaking flights. He was also, in his day, the finest *Spitfire* aerobatic pilot we shall ever see. The aircraft was ferried away to No 12 Maintenance Unit, RAF, on 25th January, 1942. By 1st April, 1942 she turned up for duty with No 401 (Canadian) Squadron, coded *YO-D*. *BL628* stayed with that unit for the following three months, after which she was re-allocated to No 308 (Krakowski) Squadron, an all-Polish unit based at RAF Northolt.

Apparently her face did not fit — or maybe it was something she'd said — for she was moved on within the week to No 167 Squadron, then at Castletown, Scotland. Some six weeks later, on the 14th October, she was again moved on, this time to No 610 (County of Chester) Squadron, Royal Auxiliary Air Force, which had also taken up residence at Castletown having just moved north from Ludham. Within six weeks *BL628* suffered her first flying accident, severe enough to require factory repairs. Restored to full health by January, 1943, she was, nevertheless, packed off to No 8 Maintenance Unit for storage, her brief operational life with the RAF behind her.

At about that time the Admiralty were taking an interest in the *Spitfire*. In September, 1942 the RAF transferred 100 *Mk Vs* to the Royal Navy on loan. Most of them were sent to Air Service training, Hamble for the fitting of 'A' frame arrester gear to permit deck landings on aircraft carriers. It has been suggested that the *Spitfire Mk Vs* which were handed over to the Royal Navy were operationally 'tired', or sub-standard for some other reason. There is no evidence to support that contention. All aircraft transferred from the RAF were withdrawn from storage in new condition, and simply modified by AST by strengthening the bottom longerons, fitting a faired hook, slinging and lashing lugs, and re-calibrating the airspeed indicator from m.p.h. to knots. Such aircraft were never known as *Seafires*, but as *Spitfires Mk VB (Hooked)*.

BL 628 was withdrawn from storage in June, 1943, modified to *Spitfire Mk VB (Hooked)* standard by General Aircraft Limited. The aircraft returned to store at RAF Lyneham on 17th August, 1943. During January, 1944, she was handed over to the tender, loving care of the Royal Navy, eventually joining No 719 Sqn of the Fleet Air Arm at St Merryn, Cornwall. In more than two years of existence *BL628* had flown for a mere seven months.

Little is known of *BL628's* existence as a naval training aircraft. She probably spent many hours in the circuit, carrying out ADDLs (Airfield Dummy Deck Landing). St Merryn, and other RN land bases, would have had flight deck markings applied to one or other of the runways. When practice was taking place a Deck Landing Control Officer (DLCO) would take up a position at the left-hand side of the threshold (as would be the case with a carrier at sea), and indicate approach instructions to aircraft by means of two circular 'bats' held at arms length. In his book *"SPITFIRE* – A Test Pilot's Story", Supermarine's one-time Chief Development Test Pilot recalls that '...in spite of the blind forward view of a *Spitfire,* it was possible, by making a carefully judged curved approach at minimum speed, to keep the bats in view and touch down neatly at the stern end of the 'deck'. The *Spitfire* had excellent lateral stability and aileron control right down to the stall and thus had what was needed for very slow approaches.'

Such training duties were often more wearing on aircraft than operational duties. Nevertheless, it would appear that *Spitfire Mk V BL628* served with the Royal Navy throughout the war. She later joined No 899 Squadron, Fleet Air Arm, based at Belfast, before returning finally to St Merryn.

In the Autumn of 1977 Lieutenant Peter Croser and Lieutenant Michael Aitchison, both of the Royal Australian Navy found the derelict remains of an aircraft in a farmyard at St Merryn. It lacked wings, engine rear fuselage and tailplane, consisting of little more than the cockpit section. There was enough there to recognise a *Spitfire*, but it was not until it had been inspected by Peter Arnold that its positive identification became known. The two Australians purchased the piece of 'scrap' and shipped it to their home country.

Once again, *BL628* is back in England, looking in much better shape than when she left. Furthermore, she has been joined by other essentials — a set of wings from Wigan, a *Seafire* cockpit section from Brownhills, a *Merlin 46* engine, and various other bits and pieces from Australia.

One day quite soon, Aerofab at Thruxton will have her out of the jigs and on her wheels — a veritable phoenix ready to rise again.

Spitfire Mk VB BL628 will fly in this country, the land of her birth, and in Australia, the land of her adoption. Good luck to her, her restorers, and all who fly in her.

SPITFIRE MK XVI, TB863
A PERSONAL INTEREST

During the ten years of my flying life which was mainly concerned with *Spitfires* (1941 to 1951), I must have flown well over 1,000 different aircraft ranging from the *Mk IA* to the *Griffon*-engined *Mk XVIII*. In one year alone — 1944 — over 600 passed through my hands as a test pilot at Casablance — and that was a 'rest' tour from operations!

Spitfires Reborn

From all that number of *Spitfires*, only one remains, as far as I know, which is just another illustration of the strange destructive urge which seems to overcome some of us in this country from time to time. That one survivor is a *Spitfire Mk XVI, TB863*. It is the only airworthy *Spitfire* in New Zealand. Its owner is Tim Wallis of Wanaka, in the South Island. As such I regard it as a tangible tribute to all the Kiwis who were such close comrades during the war years. The most noteworthy, of course, was Air Chief Marshal Sir Keith Park, victor of the Battle of Britain and Malta '42. In my case I remember, in particular, my 73 Squadron friends, Wilf Mygind, now a retired crop-duster and veteran aircraft collector whom I still see occasionally, Ted Bennett, Jock Horne and Eddie Karatau.

TB863 began service life during February, 1945, when it was delivered from Castle Bromwich to No 19 Maintenance Unit, St. Athan, South Wales. On 24th March she moved to her first operational unit, No 453 Squadron, manned by Australians and based at RAF Matlaske, Norfolk. There, she was given her first code, *FU-P.*

On her very first day with the Squadron the aircraft completed three armed reconnaissance sorties over Holland and Belgium carrying on each flight 1x500 lbs.and 2x250 lbs. high explosive (HE) bombs. Those trips set the pattern for *TB863* which operated at a high sortie rate in the short period of six weeks from initial delivery until VE-Day (8th May, 1945). By way of celebration *TB863* flew two 'victory' missions. On 2nd May she was one of twelve 453 Sqn *Spitfires* which flew escort to the RAF *Dakota (C 47)* which conveyed Queen Wilhelmina back to Holland. Six days later she had the happy task of covering British troop landings in the Channel Islands.

On 14th June No 453 Sqn. re-equipped with *Griffon*-powered *Spitfire Mk XIVs*. *TB863* was transferred to No 183 (Gold Coast) Sqn., which was probably an error as that unit was in the process of exchanging their *Spitfire Mk IXs* for *Hawker Typhoons*. Rather than hang around where she was not wanted, she was moved on to No 567 Sqn at Hawkinge, Kent.

In June, 1946, the *Spitfire Mk XVI* was re-allocated to No 691 Sqn. (later No 17 Sqn) based at RAF Chivenor, Devon. That was where I first made her acquaintance. The Squadron's task, anti-aircraft co-operation, was in itself relatively mundane to those of us who, until that point, had earned their crust in wartime front-line units. There were, nevertheless, many compensations.

The most obvious one was that we were still flying *Spitfires* — in my view much more satisfying than the *Vampires* and *Meteors* of the home-based fighter squadrons of the day. Other advantages were the magnificent area in which we worked, (I am a Devonian and will hear nothing to its detriment), the diversity of the Squadron's equipment (besides *Spitfires* we had *Beaufighters, Oxfords, Harvards, Martinets* and *Buckmasters*), and the enjoyable requirement to simulate low level target approaches and attacks.

Perhaps the most pleasing factor came from the Air Ministry policy at that time of using such squadrons as receiving units for experienced World War 2 aircrews returning to the fold after some sort of hiatus. In my case I had tried my luck as a civilian with British European Airways for a couple of years before being invited to return to the RAF permanently. I joined a collection of characters at Chivenor who will always remain in my memory. The atmosphere was as utterly different from the 'Piece of Cake' fiction as one can possible imagine. What finer comrades could one wish than Dennis White from Rhodesia, little Karel Posta, our aerobatic genius from Poland, cheerful, scruffy 'Benny' Benzinski from Prague, 'Norrie' Grove, Johnny Pearce, and the ex-wrestler from Warsaw, Frank Bernard. Keeping us all in order — or trying to — was Sqn. Ldr. Ron Noble. The names are taken at random, for there was never a trace of a misfit in No 17 Sqn..

One of the tasks which fell to us was to play the part of *Me 109s* at the 1950 RAF Display held that year at Farnborough. The item concerned the famous *Mosquito* daylight raid on the Amiens Prison, and we were to represent 'the enemy'. To make things a little more convincing we adorned our *Spitfires* with black crosses and swastikas, and had their noses daubed in yellow paint. This was done some days before the performance during which period we carried out our normal daily tasks.

Notices to Airmen — NOTAMS — had been circulated throughout the aviation world, of course, but a certain amount of confusion was undoubtedly caused in civilian circles. I recall flying *TB863*, so bedecked, on an exercise with the Royal Navy Gunnery School at Wembury, South Devon. On completion of the sortie the Controller, as he often did, asked for a low level 'fly-by' to entertain the young trainees.

I duly approached from the south, flying fast and low over the wave tops towards the Great Mew Stone, an isolated rock rising sheer out of the sea about a mile from the mainland. It was a favourite spot for longshore fishermen, and two or three boats were in the lee of the rock on this occasion.

With a sudden roar a fighter bearing all the signs of the erstwhile enemy burst into view from behind the rock bearing down upon them at a very low altitude. I will never forget the sight of their startled, upturned faces as I swept by. It occurred to me later that the fisherfolk of Devon, like everyone else, had firmly believed that the war had come to an end some years back, and nobody had told them that it had started again!

No. 17 squadron masquerade. Spitfire Mk XVI's, including TB863, representing Me bf 109's for the 1950 RAF display, Farnborough.

Just after I had left No 17 Sqn to join No 28 Sqn in Hong Kong the role of anti-aircraft co-operation was put out to civilian contract. The *Spitfire Mk XVIs, TB863* amongst them, went to Exeter to equip No 3 Civilian Ant-Aircraft Co-operation Unit (CAACU).

All went well until 17th July, 1951. On that day *TB863* blotted her copy-book when her *Packard Merlin 266* engine failed at a crucial moment on take-off, causing her to end up on her belly. Sad to say, the aircraft sustained damage of sufficient severity for her to be struck off the books.

TA863 re-emerged in 1953 (where can she have rested her wounded body in the meantime?) when she was bought by Metro-Goldwyn Meyer for cockpit scenes in the film about Douglas Bader, 'Reach for the Sky'. After shooting had been completed, the aircraft was returned to the Props Room at Pinewood Studios. She remained there, forgotten and out of sight, for a further twelve years.

As recounted elsewhere in this volume, another epic flying film involving *Spitfires* was planned for 1967 – 'The Battle of Britain'. By that time *TB863* had mysteriously lost her engine and a considerable amount of cockpit equipment. She was considered to be too far gone for renovation, even to static standard, so she was taken to RAF Henlow to be used as a 'Christmas tree' to provide spares for the other airworthy *Spitfires*.

Filming over, what was left of *Spitfire Mk XVI TB863* was put up for disposal. Her new owner, Bill Francis, moved her to his home at Southend where she remained for a further four years. In 1972, one presumes, the sight of a near-derelict *Spitfire* was beginning to pall, for the aircraft was moved down the road to the Historic Aircraft Museum at Southend Airport.

Non-airworthy she may have been, but *TB863's* travelling days were not yet done. The aircraft left Southend in 1974 to go to Duxford remaining there for the following three years. In 1977, off she went again, this time to Southam in Warwickshire.

At last, in 1982, a positive move was made in the right direction. The aircraft entered the British Civil Register as *G-CDAN*. At the same time she was moved to Personal Plane Services at Booker, near High Wycombe, where work was started on the wings. *TB863* had started her long climb back to airworthiness.

Stephen Grey assumed ownership and moved the aircraft back to Duxford in late 1985. There, David Lees removed all the internal equipment and the original skinning from the fuselage. Open to close inspection, he was gratified to see that the ribs, frames and longerons were in good condition. Everything was repainted in preparation for reskinning. The old firewall of asbestos was discarded, to be replaced by a new stainless steel construction.

Still at Duxford *TB863* was subjected to more reskinning wherever required. At the same time all the pneumatic and hydraulic plumbing was renewed. The 12-volt electrical system was updated to 24-volt, and total electrical re-wiring was carried out. Very little internal work was required to the mainplanes, but the opportunity was taken to instal extra fuel tanks in the old gun bays.

Spitfires Reborn

As 1987 drew to a close the enormous amount of work necessary to get *TB863* flying once more was almost at an end. By December, new elliptical wingtips had been manufactured and fitted. The *Merlin 266* prepared by Hovey Machine Products was installed. During the first six months of 1988 all final internal details were taken care of, a new Rotol propeller fitted, and ground runs completed.

In September 1988 the Chief Pilot of the Fighter Collection, "Hoof" Proudfoot, and Stephen Grey himself carried out eleven hours of air tests between them which resulted in the issue of a Permit to Fly.

Spitfire Mk XVI TB863 was once again licenced to fly after thirty-seven years on the ground and, at times, close to destruction.

The aircraft was crated for the long journey to New Zealand. There, she was delivered to her new owner, Tim Wallis, in time for Christmas, 1988. The aircraft was given the civilian registration of *ZK-XVI*.

Once again *TB863* was re-assembled and air tested with satisfactory results. Tim proudly flew his immaculate machine, New Zealand's only example, before the inevitable batteries of cameras. On 29th January she took off from Ardmore in the hands of her owner and headed for Masterton. This was, in fact, Tim Wallis's first cross-country flight in the aircraft. Near Waipukurau, North Island, the engine failed due to fuel starvation brought on by Tim's unfamiliarity with the fuel system. He attempted to nurse his aircraft into Waipukurau airfield, but was forced to accept a landing in a paddock short of the runway. This did not go well. For a second time in her eventful life *TB863* hit the unyielding ground ruinously hard.

Unfortunately, Tim had selected wheels down on the approach when he thought that he could make the distance. An inspection of the aircraft when it eventually arrived at Wanaka showed that the damage was even more extensive than it had appeared to be at the site of the crash.

Poor *TB863* had sunk to the ground at a high rate of descent and struck in a nose down attitude. The propeller had shattered, the spinner and the engine mounting were damaged; the oil tank, lower engine cowling and air intake were totally destroyed; one undercarriage leg had been torn out and the other nearly so; the former had pierced the wing, torn through the rear spar and damaged the flap.

The fuselage had all but broken its back when the lower longerons collapsed on impact. There was more extensive internal damage and distortion; the seat, and even the throttle, were broken. Almost the only section to escape was the tail unit. Tim Wallis had walked away from it all unscathed!

It all looked distinctly unpromising. There is no doubt that, had it been wartime with a production line going at full speed, *TB863* would have been consigned to the scrapheap. But it was not wartime, and there is no production line. Today, the intrinsic value of historic vintage aircraft is such that engineering miracles are attempted to save them when misfortune falls.

Fortunately, there is in New Zealand, an aircraft engineering facility of world class reputation called Safe Air. Indeed, it was that company's workshop supervisor, Rick Schuyl who visited Wanaka to conduct the first survey.

Safe Air faced an enormous problem as accurate costings and, therefore, the reactions of the insurers, could not be undertaken until the availability of spares from any world source was known, and a detailed repair scheme devised. Ray Mulqueen, of the Wallis team, had gained some experience of working with a Spitfire in Australia, and had assembled *TB863* at the time of its arrival in New Zealand. He immediately left for Australia to trawl for whatever bits and pieces might be available. He returned with one undercarriage leg, a new engine mount section, and an oil tank which could be used as a pattern.

This was clearly going to be a project of international proportions. Ray Mulqueen and Rick Schuyl decided to appoint the Alpinedeer Group as agents for the procurement of all the necessary spares and replacement parts, and to arrange with overseas agents for the repair of the engine and airframe parts.

So, once again, *TB863* was back 'in dock' for major surgery; the work started in June, 1989.

Safe Air's workshops fully committed from the outset. The extent of the task was even greater than the company had estimated. Over in the USA Jack Hovey, who had prepared the *Merlin 266* originally, now agreed to undertake the necessary repairs. Peter Rushen in England undertook to see to the repair of the radiators.

Spitfires Reborn

More bad news followed. It was discovered that the undercarriage spares brought in from Australia were too corroded for use. That was indeed a cruel blow which threatened to bring the whole project to a halt—had it not been for a truly amazing coincidence.

Purely by chance, Ray Mulqueen discovered that, three miles down the road from the Safe Air installation at Blenheim lived an avid collector of aviation bits and pieces called Peter Coleman. He had amassed a considerable hoard over many years. Ray wasted no time in investigating the collection.

To his delight—almost disbelief—there were two *Spitfire* undercarriage legs in good condition. More remarkable still, they both bore the same manufacturer's part number as the one destroyed in the crash. How and why those parts of an aircraft type which was itself a stranger to New Zealand skies managed to appear in the right place at the right time can only be left to the imagination. All that can be said is that, clearly, the day of miracles is not past.

Within sight of the final goal, to have *TB863* ready once again to delight the crowds at the forthcoming air shows, yet another calamity befell the project. It must have seemed as if some malignant spirit was present, determined to frustrate those who had sacrificed so much to see that the *Spitfire* would fly again. The *Merlin 266*, just back from the USA, released a tell-tale oil leak; it led to the discovery of a serious crack in the wheel casing between the supercharger and the engine.

There was only one thing for it. The wheel case had to be removed for return to Jack Hovey in the USA.

Whilst it was away, the workers in New Zealand put in a truly incredible team effort to ensure that all the outstanding work on *TB863* was completed. They worked long into the nights and sacrificed days off to get the tasks done.

Eventually, everything came together. The repaired wheel casing was refitted, and the *Spitfire* was ready for engine runs. But not until the evil spirit had produced one last fling by introducing a stray 2BA bolt into the engine coolant system! Fortunately, it was discovered before any real damage had occurred. It was removed with some difficulty after frantic telephoning to the United States to seek Hovey's advice. The engine runs were safely completed.

Spitfires and Saviours

Tim Wallis, proud ownder of New Zealand's only airworthy Spitfire — TB 863. (Labette)

On 3rd September Stephen Grey, standing by in England, received a 'phone message from Ray Mulqueen to the effect that *TB863* was finally ready in all respects for air testing.

He promptly 'scrambled' to the other side of the world.

On 7th April, 1990, the *Spitfire XVI* was flown for the first time since the accident which had almost destroyed it.

In just fifteen months, by teamwork difficult to equal in terms of dedication, skill and sheer determination not to be beaten, a forty-five year old *Spitfire*, which had been twice virtually written off, had been raised from the dead to fly again.

Unique in her country of adoption, *TB863* had been doctored back to health again by Australians, Americans, British and, above all, New Zealanders.

Just a few weeks ago I received a letter from Charles Labette of Wellington who said, with absolutely justifiable pride:

"...at Masterton ... I was able to take a few photographs of *TB863* which give an indication of the excellent repair job carried out by our friends at Safe Air Ltd., Blenheim."

Spitfires Reborn

That is a masterpiece of understatement.
Not for the first time I repeat a cry often heard during the war years..
"Well done, the Kiwis!"

This Is Not The End

...just the last page of a book. It has only been possible in the space available to select a few true stories about aircraft and people which I hope will be of general interest.

The *Spitfire* story is a very lengthy one, starting as far back as the '20s, when R J Mitchell's designs for the Schneider Trophy floatplane racers first became a reality, indicating the way towards a generation of fast, single-seater monoplane fighters. The *Spitfire* and the *Hurricane* arrived in the nick of time.

The last of the *Spitfires* were withdrawn from RAF service in the early '50s. The legend was almost allowed to die as thousands were dispersed to far away places with strange sounding names, or were sold — practically given away — as scrap metal. The classic fighter which had so recently been the torch of freedom flickered and almost died.

With the passing of the years a new generation has rekindled the flame. Once again *Spitfires* are seen at airshows in the United Kingdom, the United States, Australia, New Zealand, and Canada. It has only been possible in the space available to recount a few of the many true stories of people and machines connected with the reincarnation of the *Spitfire*, stories which I hope will be of interest to the general reading public.

But there are stories yet to come as more enthusiasts decide that they, too, can play a part in the magical world of the *Spitfire*. People like Julian Mitchell and Stephen Arnold (Peter is not related to him, either) of Kidlington, Oxfordshire. They were not born when the *Spitfire* was declared obsolete by the RAF, but they caught the bug a few years ago and got started with nothing more than a pair of metal detectors and a lot of optimism a few years ago. Starting with the shell of a *Spitfire Mk VB* fuselage (*BL370*) which they discovered in a scrap yard, they are attempting to reconstruct the aeroplane, as far as possible, from original parts. Impossible? They do not think so — and neither do I. If dedication and hard work are what is required, they will get there. They already have a collection amounting to two-thirds of the components they require. At a *Spitfire* Society

Spitfires Reborn

exhibition held at Kidlington on 20th January, 1989, Julian and Stephen proudly displayed the Rolls Royce *Merlin 45* engine which will one day — perhaps within the next ten years — power the aircraft they hope to fly themselves.

That is typical of the spirit which exists today in many younger people. It is just one of the reasons why I founded the *Spitfire* Society in 1983. It is very gratifying for first generation *Spitfire* people such as myself to see and encourage this new generation of enthusiasts in their determination to keep a legend alive.

We were the ones who almost let it die. They are the ones who will see that it doesn't.

David Green

If you would like to be put on the Brooks Books mailing list, to receive information about all our new aviation publications, together with unique special offers, then send your name and address to: Brooks Books, 23 Sylvan Avenue, Bitterne, Southampton, Hampshire, England, SO2 5JW.